FREE DVD  FREE DVD

Advanced Placement World History
DVD from Trivium Test Prep!

Dear Customer,

Thank you for purchasing from Trivium Test Prep! We're honored to help you prepare for your AP exam.

To show our appreciation, we're offering a **FREE *AP Exam Essential Test Tips* DVD by Trivium Test Prep**. Our DVD includes 35 test preparation strategies that will make you successful on the AP Exam. All we ask is that you email us your feedback and describe your experience with our product. Amazing, awful, or just so-so: we want to hear what you have to say!

To receive your **FREE *AP Exam Essential Test Tips* DVD**, please email us at 5star@triviumtestprep.com. Include "Free 5 Star" in the subject line and the following information in your email:

1. The title of the product you purchased.

2. Your rating from 1 – 5 (with 5 being the best).

3. Your feedback about the product, including how our materials helped you meet your goals and ways in which we can improve our products.

4. Your full name and shipping address so we can send your FREE *AP Exam Essential Test Tips* DVD.

If you have any questions or concerns please feel free to contact us directly at 5star@triviumtestprep.com. Thank you!

- Trivium Test Prep Team

Table of Contents

Introduction

The Advanced Placement World History course is remarkably broad, covering the historical development of the entire world from the earliest historical periods. This course spans the earliest stages of human development to the modern world and from east to west. Additionally, the course includes significant information on regions less commonly studied, including Asia, Africa, Latin America, and Oceania.

The breadth of the course poses a number of challenges for both students and teachers. While there is no set textbook for AP World History, the course is designed to mimic an introductory college world history course and most college-level world history textbooks will provide an appropriate review tool for this subject, particularly if you are planning to take the test without having taken the course. This review text is ideal for both groups of students, but should not stand alone if you have not taken the AP World History class in school.

Structure and Content

In order to make this subject more manageable, the College Board has identified a few key concepts in each historical period. This guide will be organized chronologically, with each of the key concepts clearly noted and emphasized. Each chapter will include common themes, helping you to organize information and consider how different periods and societies relate to one another. For the purposes of this course, the world will be divided into five key regions. These are:

1. Africa

2. The Americas

3. Asia

4. Europe

5. Oceania

Notably, while this course will include information about both European and American history, this is a world history class, and you should expect this course to provide a balanced look at each region.

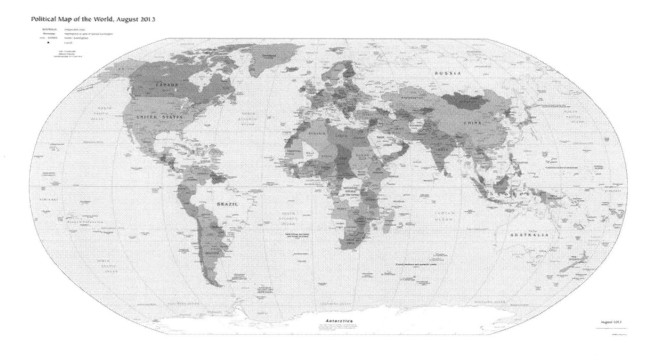

Figure 1 Map of the World[1]

Take a moment to review the map above. Africa includes the entire continent of Africa to the Isthmus of Suez. Studies of Africa will include the history of states like Egypt and Ethiopia, the history of trade and colonialism. Asia is bordered on the west by the Ural Mountains and the Isthmus of Suez. This region will include studies of varied cultures, including ancient Mesopotamia, China, Japan and India. The Americas include all of South, Central and North America. Europe is west of the Ural Mountains and includes Western, Southern, Eastern and Central Europe, while Oceania includes Australia, New Zealand and several other island states in the southernmost portion of the world.

The class will also teach four essential historical thinking skills. These skills are, according to the College Board:

- **Historical Argumentation**: By the end of the AP World History course, students should
be able to recognize, define and express a historical problem and construct an argument

---

[1] CIA World Factbook

addressing that problem using historical evidence. Students should be able to use historical evidence, including historical documents, appropriately, understanding them within their historical context.

- **Chronological Understanding**: Students should fully understand historical causation, including concepts of coincidence and correlation. They should be able to recognize the importance of events in chronological order, including both the continuity of events and cultures, as well as historical change.

- **Historical Comparison and Events in Context**: Comparison allows students to compare and discuss historical events in a single society, in a single period across multiple societies or in other ways. Context identifies how events relate to other events, culture, or things occurring globally at the same time.

- **Interpretation and Historical Synthesis**: Interpretation allows students to assess various historical viewpoints and perspectives. Synthesis brings together all aspects of historical study, including historical argumentation, chronological understanding, comparison and interpretation.

The Advanced Placement World History test consists of two parts, multiple choice questions and free response questions. The test is quite long, totaling three hours and five minutes in length. There are 70 multiple choice questions, making up 50 percent of your total grade. You'll have 55 minutes in total for this portion of the test. Each of the six historical periods of the test will be included on the multiple choice portion of the examination, with questions distributed as follows. Period 1, prior to 600 BCE, will account for three to four questions of the 70 on the test. Period 2, from 600 BCE to 600 CE, will account for 15 percent or around ten questions. Each of the remaining periods accounts for 20 percent of the test, or around 14 questions.

The free response portion of the examination takes up the majority of the test time, two hours and 10 minutes. There are three free response questions in total, but they vary widely. The first of the free response questions is a document-based question. You will have one document-based question, with 50 minutes to complete this response. This 50 minute period includes a 10 minute reading period and a 40 minute writing period. The next essay focuses on historical change or continuity, with a 40 minute total writing period. The final essay is a historical comparison, again with a 40 minute writing period. In the sample essays later in this text, you'll find examples of all the types of questions, along with sample answers in a high, average and low scoring range. For a high-scoring test, you need to do well on both the essay questions and the multiple choice questions. Plan to spend the first five minutes of each writing block planning your essay with a brief outline or some simple notes. This will help you to stay on track and focused throughout the essay. Practice will help you to write well under time pressure.

You can opt to work your way through this guide and your textbook in a straightforward fashion, from beginning to end, or you may begin by taking one of the sample tests in the back of this text. If you opt to take a sample test, grade your test and assess the questions you struggled most with, devoting additional study time to those sections. When you're preparing for the test, take the time to take at least one sample test in circumstances similar to those of the actual test day. Set a timer, work in a quiet room, and limit your access to supplementary materials. It is particularly important that you practice writing under pressure, particularly given the number of questions on the AP World History exam.

Scoring

The test is scored on a scale of 1 to 5. A score of 5 is extremely well qualified to receive college credit, while a score of one is not qualified to receive college credit. While colleges and universities use scores differently, a score of 4-5 is equivalent to an A or B. A score of 3 is approximately similar to a C, while a score of 1-2 is comparable to a D or F. The examination is scored on a curve, adjusted for difficulty each year. In this way, your test score is equivalent to the same score achieved on a different year. The curve is different each year, depending upon the test. Approximately 46 percent of students receive a 4 or 5 on the AP World History examination.

Scores of 4 to 5 are widely accepted by colleges and universities; however, scores of 3 or lower may provide less credit or none at all. More elite schools may require a score of 5 for credit and some schools vary the required score depending upon the department. You will need to review the AP policies at your college or university to better understand scoring requirements and credit offered. While you'll take the AP World History Examination in May, your scores will arrive in July. You can have your scores sent to the college of your choosing, or, if you're testing after your junior year, simply wait until you're ready to apply to the colleges of your choice.

Scoring on the multiple choice section of the examination is straightforward. You receive one point for each correct answer. There are no penalties for an incorrect answer or a skipped question. You should, if you're unsure, guess. Even the most random guess provides you a one in four chance of a point. If you can narrow down the choices just a bit, your chances increase and, along with them, your possible test score.

The FRQs are scored from 1-8 depending upon the quality of the essay. Essay questions are graded by human graders, typically high school and college psychology instructors. They have been trained to grade the essays by the College Board. You'll find more information on specifics about scoring the free response questions in the chapter that includes the sample essay questions and responses.

Staying Calm, Cool and Collected

Conquering test anxiety can help you to succeed on AP exams. Test anxiety is common and, if it's mild, can help keep you alert and on-task. Unfortunately, if you suffer from serious shakes, it may leave you struggling to focus, cause you to make careless errors, and create potential panic.

- Allow plenty of time for test preparation. Work slowly and methodically. Cramming doesn't help and will leave you depleted and exhausted.

- Remember to stay healthy. Sleep enough, eat right, and get regular exercise in the weeks preceding the AP examination, particularly if you're planning to take several tests during the same testing window.

- Practice breathing exercises to use on test day to help with anxiety. Deep breathing is one of the easiest, fastest and most effective ways to reduce physical symptoms of anxiety.

While these strategies won't eliminate test anxiety, they can help you to reach exam day at your mental best, prepared to succeed.

The night before the test, just put away the books. More preparation isn't going to make a difference. Read something light, watch a favorite show, go for a relaxing walk and go to bed. Get up early enough in the morning to have a healthy breakfast. If you normally drink coffee, don't skip it, but if you don't regularly consume caffeine, avoid it. It'll just make you jittery. Allow ample time to reach the testing location and get your desk set up and ready before the examination starts.

What to Take to the Test

- A sweatshirt or sweater, in case the testing room is cold.

- A bottle of water.

- At least two No. 2 pencils, sharpened.

- At least two black or blue ink pens.

- A wristwatch

And a quick note here: there's no need to take paper along. You'll receive not only the test booklet, but also additional scratch paper to take notes and make outlines for your free response questions. Plan to leave your phone in the car, but you may take a paperback book or magazine into the testing room if you're early.

Tackling the Test

Some people don't find testing terribly anxiety-inducing. If that's you, feel free to skip this section. These tips and techniques are designed specifically for students who do struggle with serious test anxiety and need to get through the test as successfully as possible.

- Control your breathing. Taking short, fast breaths increases physical anxiety. Maintain a normal to slow breathing pattern.

- Remember your test timing strategies. Timing strategies, like those discussed in relation to the free response questions, can help provide you with confidence that you're staying on track.

- Focus on one question at a time. While you may become overwhelmed thinking about the entire test, a single question or a single passage often seems more manageable.

- Get up and take a break. While this should be avoided if at all possible, if you're feeling so anxious that you're concerned you will be sick, are dizzy or are feeling unwell, take a bathroom break or sharpen your pencil. Use this time to practice breathing exercises. Return to the test as soon as you're able.

- Remember that, while this may be an important test, it is just a test. The worst case scenario is that you do not receive college credit and find yourself taking human geography in college. If you do so, the knowledge you gained in the AP Human Geography course will help you to succeed.

Period 1: Before 600 BCE

There are three key concepts for this region, as set forth by the College Board in the AP

World History Curriculum Framework. These are:

1. Geography and Population Distribution

2. The Neolithic Revolution

3. Societal Development and Interaction

The World before Agriculture

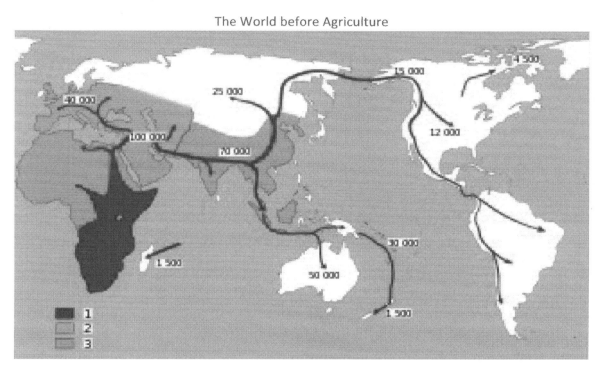

Figure 2 The map above shows early migrations. Here, green represents various types of early Hominids. The yellow-green color is representative of Neanderthals, while red lines and blocks represent modern humans.[2]

During the Paleolithic era, from around 250,000 BCE to around 8000 BCE, early humans

spread outward from Africa, moving into much of the world. The map above shows the spread

of early humans, including various types of Hominids, Neanderthals, and modern humans.

---

[2] By NordNordWest (File:Spreading homo sapiens ru.svg by Urutseg) [Public domain], via Wikimedia Commons, accessed October 19, 2015.

Early groups of humans were relatively small, surviving by hunting local animals, following animal herds, and gathering locally available plant foods. While the earliest hominids used simple stone tools, stone tool technology increased and expanded over time, allowing for improvement to hunting implements and other tools, as well as adaptations to different climate conditions. Tool technology likely played a role in the success of modern humans. While the earliest tools were likely spears and hand axes, eventually throwing spears and bows and arrows developed, providing safer and more effective ways to hunt large game.

Fire was another key technological innovation. Fire provided protection from animals, warmth, and the ability to cook food. Cooking food made both meat and plant foods more digestible and the nutrients more accessible. Evidence for the existence of fire is quite early, with wide scholarly agreement that Homo erectus had control of fire by 400,000 years ago. There is some evidence of earlier control of fire, perhaps well over a million years ago.

While early groups of humans were relatively small, likely family groups connected by kinship ties, they maintained connections with other groups, sharing goods, technology and information. It is likely that they sought mates from other groups as well. Art work and artifacts from the Paleolithic era show that they developed religious and spiritual beliefs during this time, with a particular interest in the fertility of the animals they hunted. Some spaces, including difficult to access caves, were likely particularly sacred. Religious beliefs were likely shared during meetings between kinship groups.

The Neolithic Revolution is defined by the introduction of agriculture. Agriculture includes both the intentional planting, care and harvest of plant foods, as well as pastoral care of animals. Plants were domesticated prior to animals; however, the dates for the introduction of agriculture differ widely from region to region, as do the plants and animals domesticated by each culture. Local plants and animals were the first domesticated.

While we do not have written records from this time, it is believed that the domestication of plants was gradual. At first, gatherers may have simply cared for naturally growing plants. The first form of intentional plant cultivation likely involved cuttings from tubers of various sorts. Tubers are high in carbohydrates and relatively hardy, as well as easy to grow. The process of collecting, saving and planting seeds likely came somewhat later. The first seed crops were grains of various sorts, including oats, barley, rye and types of wheat. These provided the basis for breads and porridges. Other food crops, including legumes of various sorts, came somewhat later. Gathering activities continued even after the introduction of agriculture as people relied upon known and naturally growing plants, including places where nuts or fruits grew.

The domestication of animals came later, but consisted of local animals. Both larger animals, like sheep and goats, and smaller animals, like dogs, were domesticated. Poultry, like chickens, were also domesticated, providing meat and eggs. Domesticated animals provided meat, milk and fiber. In Mesoamerica, no animals were domesticated, while in the Andes Mountains, llamas and alpacas were the only large domesticated species.

Agriculture first developed in areas with particularly rich and fertile soils, especially along river valleys. Today, it is believed that agriculture in each of these regions developed relatively independently. While some amount of cultural interaction may have been possible, for instance, between Mesopotamia and Egypt, agriculture appeared in different regions, developing independently. These included areas along the Tigris and Euphrates River in Mesopotamia, along the Nile in Egypt, near the Indus River in India and near the Yellow River in China.

Mesopotamia. Tigris and Euphrates River Valleys.	9000-8000 BCE
India. Indus River Valley.	8000-6000 BCE
China. Yellow River Valley.	6000 BCE
Egypt. Nile River Valley	3600 BCE
Mesoamerica, Andes Mountains	2500 BCE

It is critical to recognize that all of these dates are linked to the Neolithic or Agricultural Revolution. Periodization, or the dates associated with an event or historical period, may change from place to place. It would, for instance, be inappropriate to refer to 2500 BCE as Neolithic in Mesopotamia, but perfectly appropriate to refer to the same date as Neolithic in Mesoamerica. In all cases, the Neolithic is marked by the beginning of agriculture and its associated cultural and social changes.

The domestication of plants and animals changed the world in significant ways.

- Plant and animal domestication required settled villages, rather than nomadic encampments. Rather than living in cave shelters or temporary shelters built of, for instance, animal hides, settled groups built agricultural villages, using local materials to build permanent homes.

- The introduction of agriculture changed the environment. Land was now intentionally cultivated and, along with agriculture, irrigation systems were developed to bring water to the fields and the growing communities.

- Agriculture allowed for the growth of larger communities. Food supplies were more reliable and accessible, and a larger population was needed to care for fields and flocks. An increased population allowed for more specialization of labor. Specialization of labor eventually led to the growth of new classes of individuals, like priests and scribes.

- New skills, including agriculture, required the development of new forms of technology to work the soil, including, eventually, the wheel. Metal working developed in these new Neolithic communities, along with more developed wooden tools. Need also drove the development of other technology, like pottery, which provided for food storage.

- Settled communities led to a growing social hierarchy, with some individuals having more access to resources, goods and status than others.

Societies before 600 BCE

Following the introduction of agriculture, the first settlements were relatively small; however, as technology and tools improved, settlements grew in size. Farming villages became the first cities, and the home to the first political empires. These were the first civilizations. All civilizations had to have the following:

- Political, social and religious hierarchy
- Agricultural surplus
- Trading relationships with other cities
- Specialization of labor
- An army or other defense mechanisms

Civilizations grew and spread, forming states and eventually empires.

There are several early civilizations, called core civilizations, which are especially important. These first civilizations grew into early states and empires, gaining control of significant land and founding other cities. In some cases, multiple different states and empires grew out of the same core civilization. Core civilizations shared a number of traits. They were home to early religions, with monotheism developing in Hebrew-speaking regions of the Near East and the pantheon that would become Hinduism beginning in Southeast Asia. Social hierarchies increased, with the development of the ruling class, and law codes. Technology developed and spread, as individuals moved outward, often following their animals to new pastures, a process called pastoralization. Trade expanded along with territory. Below, you'll find a discussion of each of these core civilizations, as well as the states found in that civilization.

Mesopotamia

One of the key early agricultural sites, Mesopotamia, sometimes called the Fertile Crescent, is located in modern-day Iraq, extending into parts of Iran, Syria, and Turkey. This area includes the river valleys of both the Tigris and Euphrates Rivers. The first cities, including Uruk, developed in this region. These cities used both stone and mud-brick architecture, centered on a high, stepped pyramid structure, called a ziggurat, and were home to many innovations, including writing and law, particularly the law codes of Hammurabi. Rulers were closely connected to religion, and may have, in some societies, been deemed or treated as gods. Eventually, as the cities of Mesopotamia grew, it saw a series of empires and a series of conquests. You'll find these empires listed chronologically below. Do note that while the graphic illustrates the dominant state at any point in time, in fact, they may overlap, suggesting that they shared this region for a time, with one eventually victorious over the other.

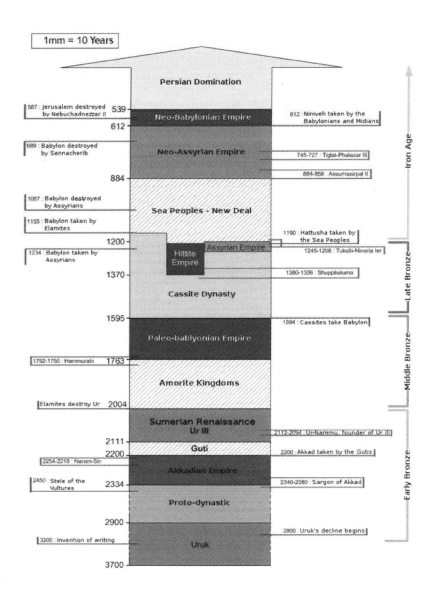

Within the figure:

1mm = 10 Years

Persian Domination

587 : Jerusalem destroyed by Nebuchadnezzar II — 539

Neo-Babylonian Empire

612 : Niniveh taken by the Babylonians and Midians

612

689 : Babylon destroyed by Sennacherib

Neo-Assyrian Empire

745-727 : Tiglat-Phalazar III

884

884-858 : Assurnasirpal II

1087 : Babylon destroyed by Assyrians

1155 : Babylon taken by Élamites

Sea Peoples - New Deal

1200

1190 : Hattusha taken by the Sea Peoples

1234 : Babylon taken by Assyrians

Hittite Empire   Assyrian Empire

1245-1208 : Tukulti-Ninurta Ier

1370

1380-1336 : Shuppiluliuma

Cassite Dynasty

1595

1594 : Cassites take Babylon

Paleo-bablyonian Empire

1792-1750 : Hammurabi — 1763

Amorite Kingdoms

Élamites destroy Ur — 2004

Sumerian Renaissance Ur III

2112-2094 : Ur-Nammu, founder of Ur III

2111

2200

Guti

2200 : Akkad taken by the Gutis

2254-2218 : Naram-Sin

Akkadian Empire

2450 : Stele of the Vultures — 2334

2340-2280 : Sargon of Akkad

Proto-dynastic

2900

3200 : Invention of writing

Uruk

2800 : Uruk's decline begins

3700

Right side labels: Iron Age, Late Bronze, Middle Bronze, Early Bronze

Figure 3 The image above illustrates a chronology of the dominant society or state in Mesopotamia, with key historical events listed. All dates are BCE.[3]

Egypt

Ancient Egypt is perhaps the best known early civilization. Centered on the Nile River Valley, the civilization of ancient Egypt is responsible for the pyramids, mummies and Sphinx that still entrance visitors today. While Egyptian culture developed gradually over thousands of years, including the development of architecture, writing or hieroglyphs, funeral practices and

---

[3] Image by Chronologie_Mesopotamie_2.png: Venal Mesopotamian_Chronology_2.png: *Chronologie_Mesopotamie_2.png: Venal derivative work: SimonTrew (talk) derivative work: Ixalarx [CC BY-SA 3.0 (http://creativecommons.org/licenses/by-sa/3.0)], via Wikimedia Commons, accessed October 19, 2015.

religion, the Egyptian history of the dynastic period is best known, beginning with the early dynastic period. Lower Egypt and Upper Egypt were united during this period. The monuments most closely associated with ancient Egypt, the pyramids, date to Old Dynasty, between 2528 and 2474 BCE. The Old Kingdom was succeeded by the Middle Kingdom and eventually the New Kingdom, until Egypt eventually fell into a period of decline under Persian rule in the 6th century BCE. While the Egyptian kingdom was united and remained largely united through much of its history, it did so with a powerful army, typically led by the Pharaoh, or Egyptian ruler. The ruler was supported by not only a military establishment, but also a religious one, with priests and scribes.

India

The great civilization of the Indus River Valley, sometimes called Harappan, is another of the early core civilizations in world history. The civilization of the Indus River Valley is most commonly represented by the great cities they created; Mohenjo-Daro and Harappa. The civilization in the Indus River Valley appeared around 3300 BCE and was thriving by 2600 BCE. Like other early civilizations, it grew from smaller agricultural communities. The cities of the Indus River Valley are particularly known for their city planning and infrastructure, including large non-residential buildings, baked brick construction, drainage and water supplies. While they did have a system of writing, it has not been deciphered, and so relatively little is known of their language. They were skilled metalworkers, and there is some evidence of the beginning of a pantheon of gods, some of which may be associated with Hinduism even today; however, evidence for religious practice and belief is scarce. Some Harappan communities continued to grow and thrive until the invasion by Alexander the Great in 325 BCE. While a few communities remain, climate change, including extreme monsoons, likely contributed to the end of the Harappan culture. Eventually, new communities were established alongside the Ganges River.

China

The Shang civilization developed in the Yellow River Valley of China. While communities had been established for some time in this region, the Shang Dynasty, sometimes called the Middle Kingdom, began around 1600 BCE and continued until 1046 BCE. The empire's capital was located near modern-day Anyang. The Shang developed writing, fine bronze working skills, and ceramics. Bronze was used for artwork, but also for weaponry. Writing survives in bronze inscriptions, as well as inscriptions on bone, found in graves and elsewhere. The civilization was organized under a single ruler, with a number of cities, each walled for defense. The Shang Dynasty was succeeded by the Zhou Dynasty in 1045 BCE. The Zhou Dynasty decentralized rule in China, eventually weakening the empire and leading to conquest. While the Zhou Dynasty continued into the third century BCE, the Western Zhou Dynasty and Eastern Zhou Dynasty are quite separate from one another. With decentralization, the Western Zhou Dynasty lasted until 771 BCE.

Mesoamerica

The Olmec civilization originated in what is now the South-Central part of Mexico. This Mesoamerican culture dates to 1500 BCE to 400 BCE. Several traits common to later Mesoamerican societies began in the Olmec civilization, including specifically Mesoamerican ball games and ritual bloodletting. The Olmec also developed the first system of writing in the Americas and the first calendars. The Olmec people are particularly known for their artwork, including colossal sculpted heads. Relatively little is known about the religious or social organization of the Olmec; however, it is believed that their cities were primarily ritual centers, rather than traditional urban areas. The majority of the population lived in smaller villages.

There is little evidence of military or political control at smaller Olmec sites and no signs of the

conquest associated with other core civilizations or later Mesoamerican civilizations.

South America

The Chavin civilization developed in the Andes Mountains, in modern-day Peru from 900

BCE to 200 BCE. The Chavin are known for several remarkable accomplishments. First, their

society did not grow up in a fertile river valley, but rather a harsh mountain climate. This led to

innovations in drainage, temperature control and irrigation. They are also some of the finest

early goldsmiths, producing work of incredible delicacy. While animals had been domesticated

in other parts of the globe for some time, the Chavin were the first to domesticate camelids, like

llamas and alpacas, still used in the Andes today. While there is evidence for a social and

religious hierarchy among the Chavin, and for their influence on other communities, there is no

evidence of war among the Chavin peoples.

Summary

- Paleolithic peoples survived by hunting and gathering. They did not live in permanent settlements, used stone tools and controlled fire.
- The Agricultural Revolution initiated the Neolithic age. The dates for the Agricultural Revolution vary widely from region to region.
- With agriculture came settlements, villages and eventually cities. With the development of cities came core civilizations.
- The Core Civilizations are: Mesopotamia, Nile River Valley, Indus River Valley, Yellow River Valley, the Olmec of Mesoamerican and the Chavin of the Andes Mountains in South America.
- Organized religion, social hierarchy, literature, and writing all developed, along with pottery, architecture and metalworking during this time.

Commonly called the Classical Era, the period from 600 BCE to 600 CE is home to many of the world's great cultures, including ancient Greece and Rome, the Qin Dynasty, the Persian Empire, the Maya and the Moche. The three key concepts identified by the College Board for Period 2 in World History are:

1. The Development of Religion
2. The Growth of States and Empires
3. The Emergence of Trade Networks

Each of these three key concepts can be found in cultures throughout the world during this period and provide a valuable framework for your study of this time. Do keep in mind that this is significant growth and development, so retain your focus on these concepts throughout your study.

Just as there are core civilizations found in Period 1, there are a number of key civilizations in Period 2.

- Persian Empire

- Qin and Han China

- Maurya and Gupta India

- Phoenician Colonies

- Greek City-States

- Roman Empire

- Mayan City-States and Teotihuacan

- Andean Moche

This is the most extensive period of religious growth, with the origins of several major religions, including Buddhism, Christianity and Confucianism dating to this period. While Hinduism and Judaism have their origins even earlier, their religion became significantly more important during this period.

Judaism

Following the Babylonian Captivity of the 6th and 5th centuries BCE, the Hebrew Scriptures were codified and written, providing a clear, shared story for the Jewish people. The Second Temple Period began in 530 BCE and lasted until 70 CE, ending with the destruction of Jerusalem by the Romans. Following the sack of Jerusalem and destruction of the Temple, the Jews dispersed throughout the world, forming smaller communities. This is called the diaspora, and is a key part of Jewish history. The written Hebrew Scriptures and shared rituals united Jews throughout varied regions. Rabbinical tradition began after the fall of the Temple, serving to organize and standardize practice, even when spread over a great distance.

Hinduism

Hinduism impacted all aspects of life in India, including both social and religious life. Hinduism is a polytheistic religion and is the oldest of the world's religions. While Hinduism may have its roots in the earliest Indian societies, the oral Vedic traditions were written, sometime before 1000 BCE, and spread throughout the region, blending aspects of different local religions. There are several key beliefs associated with Hinduism. In particular, the Hindus believed in a process of rebirth or reincarnation, based upon their deeds in this life, or karma. Eventually, the believer would reach Moksah and become one with the Great Brahman.

The caste system associated with Hinduism impacted all aspects of life for millennia. While the caste system is a form of social and religious hierarchy, it is quite defined, by birth, rather than achievement with no opportunity for change. The castes are as follows:

1. The Brahmans, made up of priests and learned individuals

2. The Kshatriyas, made up of warriors and property owners

3. The Vaishyas, made up of traders and merchants

4. The Shudras, made up of laborers

Originally, the castes impacted religious activities only, but at some time between 200 BCE and 100 CE, additional laws were put into place impacting social activities and legal regulations for each class.

Buddhism

Like Hinduism, Buddhism began in India. Founded by Siddhartha Gautama around 500 BCE, Buddhism retained some concepts found in Hinduism, including the idea of karma and rebirth. It did not acknowledge or support the caste system in religion and put forth the idea that everyone had the potential to reach nirvana, or the end of suffering. Early Buddhism did not criticize the social and political existence of the caste system.

There are "Four Noble Truths" in Buddhism. These are:

1. In life, there is suffering.

2. Suffering comes from desire.

3. Those seeking nirvana should attempt to avoid suffering.

4. This can be done by following the Eight-Fold Path.

    1. Right view

2. Right intention

3. Right speech

4. Right action

5. Right livelihood

6. Right effort

7. Right mindfulness

8. Right concentration

Buddhism does not require a belief in deity, but merely that one strive for nirvana. Theravada Buddhism is closer to Buddha's message, while Mahayana Buddhism developed later and presents a doctrine of eternal salvation. Buddhism has a long monastic tradition, commonly identified with Theravada Buddhism. Mahayana Buddhism is less monastic; however, Buddhists of all types live and work both in and out of monasteries. Buddhism spread throughout Asia along the Silk Road and other trading routes through missionary efforts.

Confucianism

Confucianism is closely associated with Chinese history, culture, politics and society. First implemented under the Han Dynasty around 500 BCE, Confucianism began as a social and political philosophy, before later incorporating more metaphysical and spiritual traits. Under the Han, Confucianism was the state ideology. Confucianism valued structure, obedience, and a strong allegiance to family. Males, particularly first sons, were especially valued, and children owed their parents obedience and support. Confucianism supported a strongly patriarchal culture with strict gender and social roles.

Daoism

Daoism developed around the same time as Confucianism and in the same place as Confucianism, China. While Confucianism emphasized a strict, human order, Daoism emphasized nature. Ancestor worship was embraced by Daoism, along with an emphasis on peace and balance. Daoism shaped Chinese beliefs about medicine, architecture, and interactions with nature.

Christianity

Christianity developed in southwest Asia, in what is today modern-day Israel, in the first century of the current era. The founder of Christianity, Jesus Christ, spread his message to a relatively small number of people; however, that message spread following his death, through missionary efforts and the Gospels. Like Buddhism, Christianity stressed spiritual equality, but Christianity promised eternal life and salvation. After several centuries of persecution in the Roman Empire, Christianity became the official state religion in the fourth century CE. Around the same time, the texts associated with Christianity, including the Old Testament or portions of traditional Jewish teaching and the New Testament, or stories of Christ's life and letters and writings of his followers, were codified. Christianity spread relatively rapidly, taking on distinctly different forms in the east and west, particularly after the fall of Rome and progressive growth of the Eastern Roman or Byzantine Empire from the 5th century onward.

Animism and Shamanism

Animism and Shamanism remained common, particularly in more rural or isolated areas, outside the reach of the growing empires and off of trade routes. While these are distinct, they may coexist. Animism is the belief that all things, including inanimate objects, have a spirit. Shamanism is the belief that a few individuals have special access to a spirit realm or special powers. Ancestor worship was common in both belief systems.

The Growth of Culture

Art, architecture, painting, sculpture, poetry, drama, literature, and history all flourished between 600 BCE and 600 CE. Cultures around the globe developed new cultural traditions and carried on old ones. While this course cannot provide you with a comprehensive look at the development of art, literature and culture around the world, you should, for the purposes of the AP World History examination, be aware of a few key trends and achievements of this period.

Literature and Drama

- Greek drama developed during this time, probably from earlier oral traditions, including songs and storytelling. Moral dramas, like the well-known story of Oedipus, were among the earliest plays; however, comedies followed.

- The Greeks took a strong interest in history, both their own and that of others. Herodotus is widely recognized as one of the most important of these early historians, providing information about sites around the known world at the time.

- Indian epic poetry, like the Bhagavad Gita, told stories from the Hindu faith.

Architecture

Characteristic architectural styles developed throughout the world during this period. Below, you'll find a summary of some of these.

- Greece and Rome developed planned, organized and geometrically constructed buildings, typically using post-and-lintel construction. Later, the Romans mastered the arch, and even domes. The Greeks build monumental buildings in stone, while the Romans used stone or concrete. In Greece, the Athenian Acropolis, including the Parthenon, exemplifies the style, while in Rome, grand buildings like the Pantheon are especially representative.

- In India, the Stupa was the primary religious building form. The stupa was originally a simple mound; however, over time, became complex and ornate, with multiple stone mounds built up at a single site. Rock and cave based structures also date to this time, many elaborately decorated with religious artwork.

- In Mesoamerica, early civilizations built large pyramids as religious sites. These were stepped pyramids, frequently elaborately decorated with stone sculpture. Sites are located throughout Central America.

- In China, buildings featured sloped roofs to help them blend into the environment better, and were often influenced by Daoist thought.

Artwork

- Greco-Roman artists mastered the depiction of the human body in movement. Following Alexander the Great's conquest of Persia and India, aspects of the more dramatic art of the east became influential, creating the Hellenistic style.

- Artwork throughout India and Southeast Asia was primarily religious in nature, with depictions of the Buddha, stories from the life of the Buddha, or scenes of Hindu deities or Indian epics.

- In China, landscape painting expressed the Daoist appreciation for nature.

This is the period of empire building, with many leaders acquiring significant land and power. City-states were essentially independent nations, made up of a city and its colonies, sometimes quite some distance away. While the city was at the center, it could be quite powerful and influential, but typically held relatively little land. Empires had a single ruler and held power over a substantial amount of land. The empire could continue to exist through different ruling dynasties, as occurred in China. It is especially important to recognize that these various powers, both city-states and empires not only knew of one another, but interacted as enemies, allies and trading partners.

- Empires required bureaucracy to support the individual ruler, including various support staff, generals, governors, scribes, and accountants.

- Classical governments, particularly that of ancient Athens, influenced modern democracy.

Persian and Parthian Empires of Southwest Asia

Located in Southwest Asia, the Persian Empire was centered in modern-day Iran. During the period from 550 BCE to 330 BCE, the Persian or Achaemenid Empire ruled over a great deal of land, from Western India through all of Turkey, nearly to the border of modern-day Greece. The Persian ruler relied upon lower level governors, or satraps, to manage individual regions. While conquered by Alexander the Great in 330 BCE, a new empire, the Parthian, took hold around 250 BCE and continued until 220 CE.

- Key Innovation: The Persian highway system allowed the army, traders and messengers to move with ease throughout the Persian Empire.

•

Qin and Han China

Between 500 and 220 BCE, China was not a united empire, but rather a number of warring states. This is referred to as the Warring States period. China was finally united under the first Qin dynasty ruler in 220 BCE, marking the beginning of the Qin dynasty. The Qin were legalistic rulers, who believed that they ruled with a mandate from heaven, or were divinely chosen to rule. Obedience was essential, and punishments for any failure, accidental or intentional were harsh. The Qin dynasty lasted less than 20 years and in 206 BCE, the long-lasting Han dynasty began. The Han dynasty blended Confucianism and legalism in its rule and remained in power until around 220 CE.

- Key Innovations: New canal system connected different parts of China, work on the Great Wall of China begun.

Maurya and Gupta India

There were two great empires in India in this period, the Mauryan, from 321-185 BCE, and the Gupta, from 320-550 CE. While the Mauryan Empire was relatively long-lasting, the best known ruler is Ashoka. Recognized for his conversion to Buddhism, Ashoka promoted Buddhism through monasteries and missionaries, and was known as an unusually humane ruler. The Gupta Empire, located in what is today Northern India, is best known for a number of cultural and intellectual achievements. Together, these are called the "Classical Indian Empires".

- Key Innovations: Spread Buddhism into East Asia.

- Key Innovations: The number zero, "Arabic" numerals, the game of chess.

Phoenician Colonies

The Phoenician Colonies originated along the Mediterranean Sea, in what is today Lebanon. Theirs was an empire based on money, rather than might. They were skilled mariners, establishing colonies throughout the Mediterranean and were among the best traders of their time. They primarily traded in luxury goods, like cinnamon. Carthage, a Phoenician colony in North Africa, eventually went to war with Rome.

- Key Innovations: Provided the alphabet and coinage adopted by the Greeks.

Greek City-States

The Greek city-states thrived between 600 BCE and 330 BCE. Each city-state existed independently, with its own customs, government and patron deities. They shared a common language and religion. The city of Athens was the world's first democracy; however, other city-states ranged from democracies to oligarchies to monarchies. The Greek city-states were united under Alexander the Great in 330 BCE, ending their existence as independent political entities. Alexander united much of the known world in a short-lived empire. Alexander founded the city of Alexandria.

- Key Innovations: Democracy, drama, architecture.
- Key Innovations: After Alexander the Great; Hellenism and Hellenic culture.

Roman Empire

The Roman Empire idolized and embraced the culture of Classical Greece. While Rome eventually conquered Greece, it retained its appreciation for Greek culture and history. Roman history is divided into the Roman Classical Era from 500 BCE to 30 BCE and the Roman Empire, from 30 BCE to 476 BCE. Keep in mind that these two periods should not be confused. In broad terms, everything prior to the death of Julius Caesar is the "Classical Roman Era" or Roman Republic, and everything after is the Roman Empire. The Romans expanded their empire through military strength, but also infrastructure. They built roads, aqueducts, and fortresses. Roman colonies throughout the Empire were home to people from all over the known world at the time. After the fall of Rome in 476, the Roman Empire continued, in the east. The city of Constantinople, now called Istanbul, in Turkey, was the center of this Eastern Roman Empire, which held onto the culture, skills and learning lost in the west after the fall of Rome. Called the Byzantine Empire, this Eastern Roman Empire produced thorough law codes and is the home to Eastern Orthodox Christianity.

- Key Innovations: Aqueducts, warfare, concrete.

Mayan City-States and Teotihuacan

Mesoamerican cultures developed well away from the influences of cultures found in Africa, Asia and Europe. In Mesoamerica, the dominant culture in the period from 100 CE to 900 CE was the Maya. The Mayans were city-builders, creating large cities with monumental architecture, including tall, ziggurat-like pyramids. The city of Teotihuacan existed at the same time; however, while geographically close, it was not a Maya city. The two cultures occasionally clashed and often traded with one another. Maya cities were significantly smaller than Teotihuacan, with a population of, at maximum, around 50,000 in the city and another 50,000 just outside it, in comparison to some 200,000 residents. They shared similar religious beliefs, social hierarchy and architecture. These Mesoamerican groups practiced human sacrifice.

- Key Innovations: Math, writing, calendars, astronomy.

•

Andean Moche

The Moche Empire in the Andes Mountains of South America, dating to 100 CE to 800 CE, lived along what is today the coast of Peru. The Moche built cities around pyramid-like structures, used complex irrigation systems and terracing, and traded with neighboring groups. The Moche were led by a class of warrior-priests and there was an established social hierarchy.

- Key Innovations: The Moche are best known for their remarkable artwork.

Why Did Empires Fall?

You may have noticed an end date for each of these empires. Empires fell for a variety of reasons.

- Internal reasons, including lack of authority, corruption, revolt or disease.
  - Han Dynasty
- External forces, including war and conquest.
  - Greek city-states, Rome
- Environmental forces, including famine.
  - Mesoamerica
  - Moche

These great empires were not disconnected from one another. In fact, they maintained elaborate trade relationships, buying and selling both luxury goods and raw materials.

- Raw materials included stone and lumber. For instance, Egyptian boats were made from lumber imported from elsewhere in Africa.

- Luxury goods included both manufactured goods, like silk fabric, and natural ones, like gemstones and spices.

Trade networks shared goods between different places, sometimes many thousands of miles apart, but also spread religion, technology, learning and culture. These trade networks also served as disease vectors, spreading contagious illness through large areas, including, eventually, the Bubonic Plague or Black Death. Trading networks are particularly relevant for Africa, Europe and Asia. While trade occurred in the Americas, it was on a smaller and more local scale.

Trade Networks

Trade relationships develop because people, most often the elite, want goods that are not naturally available in their area. These may be foods, luxury items, or raw materials of various sorts. Several factors influence the development of trade networks. These are:

- Geography—Geographical features may define routes and access to different locations. These include rivers, seas, mountains, and deserts.

- Climate and Resources—These determine the location of desirable natural resources, like minerals, salt, or metals.

- Safe Passage—Merchants need to be able to move goods with relative ease and safety.

Merchants and traders moved goods from place to place using trade networks. A single merchant might deliver his goods to an interim location, where he would be paid and they would move on to be transported to another destination, before the trade was completed. In other cases, merchants moved their goods themselves from place to place.

The Silk Road

While goods were often moved by river and sea, they were also taken over land. The best known land trade route was the Silk Road, but it was not the only one. The Silk Road moved East to West, while other trade routes moved North to South. While the Silk Road was named for silk, other goods were also moved, caravan-style, along this long road. Goods came from all parts of Africa, Asia and Europe to be moved along the Silk Road. East Asian traders dealt in horses, porcelain, perfume, spices, furs, ivory, and, of course, silk. Spices, rice and cotton came from South Asia, while dates, fruits, almonds and horses came from Central Asia. From Europe and the Mediterranean, traders carried glass, furs, goldwork, cattle and oils. Information, culture, and religion were shared by those who traveled these trade routes.

Sub-Saharan Africa

Trade in Sub-Saharan Africa originated in the port Cities of North Africa, along the Mediterranean Sea. These regions were rich in resources, but traders also moved south and into the Sahara Desert. These traders carried goods from these resource-rich Mediterranean areas, as well as goods from the Silk Road. They brought out slaves, gold, salt, ivory and animal skins. These items were then traded along the Silk Road as well. The introduction of the camel improved trade options throughout West Africa and Southwest Asia.

North-South Routes

North-South routes met up with the Silk Road and other East-West routes, allowing trade to extend in all directions. These routes integrated the Black Sea of Russia into the trade networks of the Classical Era. Constantinople, the capital of the Byzantine or Eastern Roman Empire, was at the juncture of many of these routes, making it a key center for trade and mercantile activity.

Sea Trading Networks

While the Silk Road and other land-based trade routes were important, they were not the only way goods and people moved from place to place. Many traders and merchants moved their goods by sea, rather than over land.

The Black Sea and the Mediterranean

One of the most ancient trade networks, the traders that sailed the Mediterranean moved goods between some of the largest and most important cities in the classical world. This trade network first developed among the ancient Egyptians and was continued throughout the Classical period. Varied goods were traded, including those that grow well in the Mediterranean, like olives and wine. Goods came out of other regions, including Africa, to the Mediterranean route and into Greece, Turkey and other regions. The Mediterranean Trade Route was largely responsible for the spread of Christianity.

The Indian Ocean Trade Network

The largest sea-based trade network was the Indian Ocean Trade Network. The Indian Ocean connected Southeast Asia, China, the Middle East and Africa through their port cities.

From these ports, goods could move to other sites either via water or land. Buddhism and later, Islam, spread through these trade routes. Sailors relied upon natural wind currents to plan their journeys. Many of the same goods traded along the Silk Road were traded on the Indian Ocean.

Trade in the Americas

Trade in the Americas was relatively limited, largely due to a several factors, listed below. Trading was primarily relatively local and involved smaller quantities of goods, including plants, animal skins and clothing.

- Smaller populations

- Lack of trading technologies, including the wheel

- Limited use of pack animals, while dogs, llamas, and alpacas were available, they did not pull large loads

- Difficult terrain, including jungles

Summary

- Major world religions were codified (Judaism, Hinduism) or developed (Buddhism, Christianity) during this period.

- Trade routes spread religion, particularly missionary religions, like Buddhism and Christianity.

- City-states ruled over a single state or multiple colonies of that state.

- Empires ruled large areas of territory, under the control of a single ruler.

- City-states and empires interacted through trade networks, sharing information, culture and technology.

The Post-Classical Era begins after the fall of Rome and the rise of the Byzantine Empire and continues through the Middle Ages. In much of the world, the most critical historical development in this period is the beginning of Islam, while in China, the Song and Tang Dynasties began, grew and thrived.

These years are marked by several distinct trends and key concepts, as defined by the College Board.

1. Expansion of Trade

2. New Forms of Community and State Formation

3. Increased Productivity Economically

This is a period of remarkable growth, economically, culturally, and politically. Empires rose and fell during the period between 600 CE and 1450 CE. While this period falls before the changes of the colonial era that follows, it is, along with those that follow, a significant focus of the AP World History examination.

Communication and Trade

While trade routes developed during the Classical Era of 600 BCE to 600 CE, these routes

grew, expanded and became ever more important in the Post-Classical Era, from 600 CE to 1450

CE. These trade routes included the Silk Road, the Indian Ocean Network, the Trans-Saharan

Network, and the Mediterranean Network. Additional trade routes also developed, taking

advantage of improved technology that allowed for faster travel. Trade of luxury items, in

particular, increases. During this time, trade in the Americas increased somewhat, although

remained less important than in Africa, Asia and Europe.

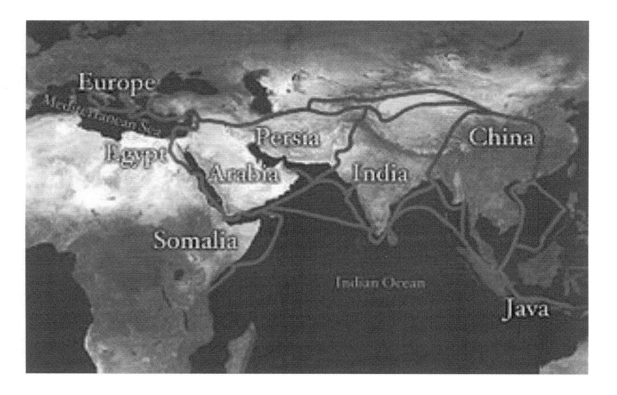

Figure 4 The map above shows both land and sea routes commonly used for trading in this period.[4]

Both land and sea trade improved with technological innovations during this time. Land

trade improved with the use of caravan organization. Caravans allowed groups of merchants to

---

[4] Map by By Whole_world_-_land_and_oceans_12000.jpg: NASA/Goddard Space Flight Center derivative work: Splette (talk) NASA - Visible Earth, images combined and scaled down by HighInBC (20 megabyte upload limit) NASA VIsible Earth [Public domain], via Wikimedia Commons, accessed October 19, 2015.

travel together for safety, taking advantages of services, like inns or caravanserai, which appeared along the route to resupply food and other necessities as they travelled. Camels were the most common choice for caravans, as they could travel long distances with limited water, ideal for the harsh conditions along the Silk Road. Camel saddles, developed during this time made camels more usable for transportation. Caravans allowed smaller merchants to transport goods and allowed for increased trade overall. Sea trade was also improved with the use of new technology. Improved navigation, using the compass and astrolabe, were key; however, ship building techniques also improved during this period.

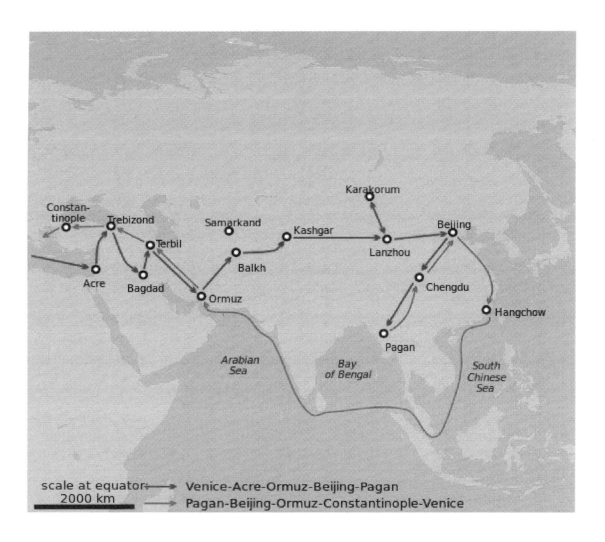

Figure 5 The map above illustrates the travels of Marco Polo in the 13th century, including many trade ports and cities.[5]

New centers of trade developed in response to the growing network of traders and accessibility of both land and sea transport. These cities grew up along trade routes, often becoming centers of not only trade, but culture as well. Below, you'll find a list of some of these key trading ports and cities. You should make certain that you know at least some of these for the exam.

- Europe- Novgorod, Constantinople (land and port), Venice (port),

---

[5] By Asie.svg: historicair 20:31, 20 November 2006 (UTC) derivative work: Classical geographer (Background map is Asie.svg) [CC BY-SA 3.0 (http://creativecommons.org/licenses/by-sa/3.0)], via Wikimedia Commons, accessed October 19, 2015.

- West Africa-Djenne, Timbuktu, Gao

- Southwest Asia-Baghdad, Tyre (port), Hormuz (port)

- Central Asia-Bukhara, Samarkand

- East Asia-Chang'an, Dunhuang, Hangzhou (port), Guangzhou (port)

- East Africa-Zanzibar (port), Kilwa (port)

- South Asia-Calicut (port), Goa (port)

- Southeast Asia-Melaka (port)

Trade is further advanced by new systems of banking. These allow lines of credit, improved currency options, and even the ability to, essentially, write a check drawn on a bank account at another location. Coinage and even paper money were used during this period, both by buyers and sellers.

While traders were of all nationalities, you should be aware of several political trends that impacted trade in various ways. One of the most critical is not involvement, but a lack of involvement. Governments, including China, allowed trade to remain unregulated in the Indian Ocean. Traders created their own systems of control and regulation in this region. In other cases, political conditions had more impact. For instance, the Silk Road was much less widely used during periods of political instability in China, and more widely used during the Han Dynasty, then later in the Song and Tang Dynasties. The Chinese government under the Tang and Song Dynasties acted to protect and encourage trade. In the Mediterranean, the Byzantine government was more actively involved in trade. Land routes across parts of Africa and Asia were under the protection of the Muslim Caliphates and later the Mongol Empire, providing safe transit, sometimes with force as needed.

Cultural Interactions, Migration and Communication

These trade relationships led to a variety of other forms of interaction. Religions spread along these trade networks, and individuals, families and groups migrated, creating communities of foreign nationals in other countries. Written language grew and developed in response to the need for communication between various groups and spoken languages changed in response to new immigrants and new linguistic exposures.

- Diasporic communities were groups of foreign nationals living in another country. Examples include: Jewish communities, Muslim communities in the Indian Ocean region and Chinese communities in Southeast Asia. Diasporic communities helped to spread other cultures and encouraged migration.

Christianity, Buddhism and Islam all spread through the trade networks. In the prior chapter, we discussed the spread of Buddhism and Christianity along these trade networks. Christianity now dominated all of Western Europe and the Byzantine Empire, with pockets of Christianity elsewhere, particularly along the Mediterranean coast. Buddhism had spread into China, Korea and other regions of East Asia by this period. The spread of these religions continued; however, they were joined by a new religion, Islam. Islam developed in modern-day Saudi Arabia and rapidly spread through surrounding regions. Within its first hundred years, Islam had gained not only religious power, but also political power, in the form of the Muslim Caliphates, centered in not only Saudi Arabia, but also modern-day Iraq. The initial expansion of Islam was military in nature; however, later, it was spread by merchants along the trading routes. The practice of religion was impacted by these cross-cultural interactions of various sorts. As religions were adopted in different regions, they developed into different sects, for instance, Sunni and Shi'ite Islam.

- Syncretism refers to the blending of different elements to create a new and cohesive whole. In historical terms, this commonly refers to religions. For instance, as Buddhism spread, it adopted some of the gods and practices of Southeast Asia, creating Mahayana Buddhism. Christianity converted sacred pagan shrines and deities into saints and holy sites, while Islam offered tolerance to "religions of the book," specifically Christianity and Judaism, but typically extended to Hinduism and Buddhism.

Stable trade routes allowed some individuals to travel, learning about other regions through personal experience. In the west, the best-known of these interregional travelers was the Italian Marco Polo. Marco Polo visited East Asia, spending a number of years living abroad and wrote about his experiences in a popular text. Other travelers include Ibn Battuta and Xuanzang.

Trade routes were not the only factor that impacted the changing cultures of this time. In Europe, the Vikings in the northern-most regions of Europe developed impressive sea-faring technologies; however, they were less interested in trade and more interested in conquest. Vikings, called Norsemen or Normans, colonized Britain, Greenland, Iceland, France, Russia, and even North America. Eventually, their influence remained in all but North America. Other groups also relied upon innovations to assist their ability to acquire land. Muslim Arabs used camels for transportation, allowing them to gain trade success, even in inhospitable regions, while the Mongols mastered the horse.

Languages spread during this period. In Europe, the Romance languages, including Italian, Spanish, and French developed into clear, vernacular languages, distinct from one another. In Africa, Bantu-speaking groups migrated into East and Southeast Africa. Eventually, the Bantu language and its variants became the predominant language family throughout the region. Bantu-speakers also brought agriculture, animal herding and technology out of Central Africa and into more distant regions.

Literary, artistic and cultural trends spread along trade routes, through missionaries and through interactions with other groups of people. In Western Europe, interactions with Islam, both peaceful and through the Crusades, brought lost knowledge from the ancient World back to the west, preserved in the libraries and universities of Islamic states. Some examples include foods, like pasta. Pasta, while typically connected to Italy, originated in China and was brought to Italy by travelers who had visited the east. Technology also spread, including paper-making, printing, and various forms of agricultural technology, like new ways to grow rice, that moved from China to Southeast Asia.

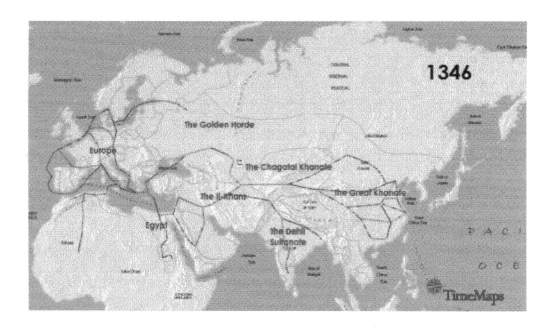

Figure 6 This illustrates the spread of the bubonic plague through much of the known world.[6]

One of the most historically important occurrences of this period also spread along the trade routes. The Black Death, or plague, of the 14th century impacted the entirety of Europe,

---

[6] By Timemaps (Own work) [CC BY-SA 3.0 (http://creativecommons.org/licenses/by-sa/3.0) or GFDL (http://www.gnu.org/copyleft/fdl.html)], via Wikimedia Commons, accessed October 19, 2015.

Asia, and parts of Africa. It moved along trade routes, often spread by rats. While plague is most often associated with bubonic plague, marked by large blisters or buboes, the same bacteria can cause a respiratory illness, spread from person to person and an infectious illness in the gut. In many regions, as much as 30 to 50 percent of the population died during the Black Death, and approximately 25 percent of the world population.

The Post-Classical Era witnessed significant political change. They revitalized old empires, creating new political structures more appropriate for their changing world, particularly in Africa, Asia and Europe. These new government structures combined traditional sources of authority with newer and more innovative ones.

- Traditional sources of authority include patriarchy, religion and land ownership.
- Innovations include new systems of taxation, the adaptation of religious institutions, and tributaries.

Western Europe

After the fall of Rome, the Catholic Church was the sole unifying force remaining in Europe. Political control, prior to 700, was in the hands of small local lords. By 800, Charlemagne had united much of Europe, including France, Germany and Northern Italy as a single empire. His empire splintered after his death, leading to the creation of a number of different kingdoms. These, particularly France and Britain, gained power throughout the Middle Ages. While some parts of Western Europe were ruled by a single ruler, other areas, including Italy, were made up of individual city-states, sometimes with a more democratic form of government.

The Byzantine Empire

The Byzantine Empire, centered in Constantinople, was already a growing power before the fall of Rome in 476 CE; however, it gained both power and prominence after the fall. From the 7th century onward, the Byzantine Empire was often in conflict with Muslim Empires to the south. The Byzantine Empire had strong religious and cultural history and maintained an active role in trade throughout this period. Eventually, weakened by conflict with Muslim Caliphates, the Byzantine Empire fell to the Muslim Ottoman Empire.

Muslim Empires

Islam began in Southwest Asia. The start of Islam is dated to 610 CE, the date when Muhammad received his first prophecy from Allah. By the end of Muhammad's life, the new Islamic religion was growing rapidly. Islam is centered on the religious text, the Qu'ran and requires Five Pillars. These are:

1. Shahadah: declaring there is no god except God, and Muhammad is his prophet.
2. Salat: ritual prayer five times a day, performed facing Mecca
3. Zakat: giving 2.5% of one's savings to the poor and needy (the requirements for Zakat are higher for non-Muslims living in a Muslim area)
4. Sawm: fasting and self-control during the holy month of Ramadan
5. Hajj: pilgrimage to Mecca at least once in a lifetime

Islam united diverse peoples across the Arabian Peninsula, before spreading out of the region and beyond. By the early 8th century, Muslims controlled Spain and were pushed back from France at the Battle of Tours in 732. By the middle of the 8th century, Muslims controlled Southwest Asia, North Africa, Spain and parts of India and Pakistan. While a single religion predominated throughout this large geographic area, there were a number of different governments, called Caliphates.

- The Umayyad Caliphate ruled in Spain, with a stable and educated empire.

- The Abbasid Caliphate, with its capital in Baghdad, ruled a large area, extending from modern Turkey into North Africa and Central Asia. The Abbasid Empire is frequently referred to as the Golden Age of Islam.

- The Delhi Sultanates ruled over Muslim portions of India and Pakistan.

The Crusades were one of the most significant political struggles of this period. Beginning in the 11th century, Christians from both Western Europe and Byzantium sought to push back Muslim forces, regain control of lands lost, and take control of parts of Southwest Asia. The

Crusades were motivated by both religious desires and economic ones, as the Byzantine Empire did not want to lose its trading interests. While the Crusades were an economic and cultural success for Western Europe, actual gains in terms of land were relatively short-lived and minimal.

Chinese Dynasties

After the fall of the Han Dynasty, China was no longer united. A number of different regional rulers gained control. Eventually, the Sui Dynasty united the country; however, it was soon followed by the Tang and eventually the Song Dynasties.

- The Sui Dynasty, from 581 to 618 CE, continued significant building projects, including canals linking the rivers of China and the Great Wall, as well as the civil service examinations that would remain a key part of Chinese government.

- The Tang Dynasty, ruling from 618 to 907 CE, continued work on building projects, rejected Buddhism, reaffirmed Confucianism, and was responsible for some of the finest art in Chinese history. The empire grew in this period before the dynasty fell to disease and famine.

- The Song Dynasty (960 to 1279 CE) encouraged trade, embraced Neo-Confucianism, which combined elements of Confucianism, Daoism and Buddhism, and implemented foot-binding, reducing the power and ability of women.

In the Tang and Song Dynasties, China gained significant cultural power over surrounding lands, a process called Sinification. Korea was briefly under the political control of China, but later made payments in exchange for political freedom. This led to lasting cultural influences, particularly Buddhism, architecture and writing. While Confucianism was not widely adopted, it was practiced among the elite classes. Japan voluntarily adopted some elements of traditional Chinese culture during this period as well, including writing and political bureaucracy. While the Chinese invaded Vietnam, they were not welcomed.

The Mongols

The Mongols gained control of much of Asia and Eastern Europe from the 13th century to the 15th century CE. The Mongols were pastoral peoples, moving their herds of sheep, goats, horses, yaks and cattle from place to place on horseback. It is this very skill on horseback that enabled their effective military strategies. Smaller leaders gained power, until eventually, Genghis Khan came to power. He pushed his troops south and into China, bringing an end to the Song Dynasty in China. The Mongols made Beijing their capital city, eliminated traditional bureaucracy, and placed power in the hand of efficient Muslim leaders. After conquering China, the Mongol Horde, called the Golden Horde by the Russians, Genghis Khan's army, moved west into Persia. Some cities surrendered, limiting violence; however, when cities or areas resisted, resistance was squashed rapidly and bloodily. The Abbasid Empire ended under the Mongolian Conquest. His victories extended as far west as Eastern Europe and Israel, through China and into modern-India.

While conquest was bloody, conditions under Genghis Khan's rule were so peaceful that trade in this time thrived under the Pax Mongolia. The huge empire was divided into a number of smaller Khanates, each with power over a set region. While the Mongol Conquest was known for its violence, under the Khanates, religious tolerance was promoted, and life was stable. In China, the Yuan Empire was established by Genghis Khan's grandson Kublai Khan.

African Kingdoms

Africa was also home to a number of powerful kingdoms, some Christian and some Muslim, depending upon the region.

- Southwest Africa was largely Muslim, home to Ghana, Songhay and Mali. These kingdoms were known for their strong roles in trade and commerce. Called Sudanic States, these kingdoms were also centers of education and culture during this period.

- Ethiopia was a significant Christian kingdom, known for its exports of coffee, especially valued in the Islamic world.

Economic growth led to remarkable changes in agriculture and technology, as information was shared between different regions. Changing agriculture and manufacturing impacted the world in a number of different ways, with an impact far beyond the immediate change caused by innovation.

Food Supply

As you learned in Period 1, an improved food supply changes life in various ways, including increasing the population and allowing for more specialization of labor.

- Food supplies in China increased with the introduction of a quicker-ripening rice from Vietnam. This allowed for more rice production per year, making rice a staple food.

- The Aztecs in Mesoamerica developed a distinctive and successful agricultural system. The chinampas were large, man-made islands constructed to grow corn and other crops. The people built platforms using woven reeds, topped them with mud, and planted them. There was no need for irrigation.

- Food production in Europe increased with the addition of horseshoes, the horse collar and crop rotation. Crop rotation helped to replenish the soil. These innovations came about through contacts with Asia and the Muslim world.

A growth in agriculture changed how agricultural labor was managed. With new agricultural technology, many farmers produced food for sale, rather than their own use, or subsistence farming.

Agricultural laborers can typically be divided into three groups.

1. Slaves have no rights or freedoms, may be bought or sold, and are personal property. Slaves could be captured and sold, be prisoners of war, or be local individuals. Slaves predominantly came from Africa and Eastern Europe.

2. Serfs have limited freedoms, are considered coerced labor, and often are connected to an owner or a piece of land.

3. Free peasants rented or owned land and worked it.

The mita system in the Andes was similar to other forms of forced or coerced labor and was later adopted by colonizing forces, including the Spanish. Forced labor was used for building projects in China; however, in Europe, tradesmen, including builders, were typically free. Serfdom declined in Western Europe, but remained in Russia and Japan for significantly longer.

Manufacture

With access to key trade routes secured, many regions began manufacturing goods of various sorts for export to different countries. Most of these were relatively small and quite valuable, making them ideal to transport over long distances. China produced porcelain, including figurines and dishes, as well as silk for export. Persia exported rugs, ceramics, Islamic religious items, including artwork, glass and silk. India exported cotton.

Urbanization

Cities declined with the fall of stable empires, as people moved from cities back to the countryside. As stable and efficient governments gained power, people moved from the countryside to the cities, a move supported by improved food supplies. Several factors increased the rate of urbanization.

1. Improved climate

2. Improved food supplies

3. Better and safer trade routes

4. Changing political structures

Cities grew dramatically, developing in significant ways during the Post-Classical era.

The increase in population and size of cities was a global phenomenon. Below, you'll find a list of several major cities and key information about each.

- In China, Chang'an and Hangzhou were especially well-developed. Chang'an was the political capital of the Han dynasty, while Hangzhou was a key trading center with many public facilities, including theaters.

- In Mesoamerica, Tenochtitlan had a civic and religious function. Positioned in the middle of a large lake, Tenochtitlan had a population of around 150,000.

- Venice was a significant center of trade, exporting glass and Christian artwork. With close ties to Constantinople, the city was well-known and proved to be one of the most important European ports.

Social Status and Gender

Essential social structures in this period included caste, class and gender. In the caste system, discussed in previous chapters, there was no room for advancement. Contrary to this, in the Christian Byzantine Empire and Muslim Ottoman Empire, individuals could rise from a low status at birth to a high one in the military or political bureaucracy. Opportunities for advancement were less in Western Europe, but there were some, particularly in the merchant guilds.

Throughout much of this period, with rare exceptions, women had few rights. China remained strongly patriarchal, as a result of the influence of Confucianism. Muslim traditions limited the rights of women across Muslim lands, commonly referred to as a whole as Dar-Al Islam. In China, Vietnamese and Mongolian women retained some amount of personal power, while in the west, some women found power through their role in the church or as a royal regent for a young son; however, this was exceptional rather than typical.

Summary

- Trade was of essential importance during this period. Key trade routes included the Silk Road, moving from East to West. Be sure you know major trade cities and goods.
- Trade spread religion, language and culture from place to place. Diasporic communities existed in some trading centers.
- New ruling governments appeared, including the Byzantine Empire, the Ottoman Empire, the Islamic Caliphates, the Tang and Song Dynasties.
- Changes in agriculture and manufacturing led to larger and more advanced cities and a greater population in the cities.
- The Black Death of the 14th century decimated much of Africa, Asia and Europe.

Period 4: 1450 CE to 1750 CE

This is a period of, for the first time, truly global history. The two halves of the world were now aware of one another and interacting with one another. Trade networks and political interactions now included not only Europe, Africa and Asia, but also Oceania and the Americas. As in times prior to this period, networks between communities, countries and regions led to the spread of goods, culture, religion and disease. These interchanges impacted all every country and continent in a variety of ways, changing their societies, altering their economies and even changing their physical environments.

The three key concepts identified by the College Board for the period between 1450 and 1750 CE are:

1. Global Networks of Trade and Communication

2. Modes of Production and Types of Social Interaction

3. The Expansion and Consolidation of Empires and Governments

Western history has traditionally remembered the years between 1450 and 1750 as a period of discovery and conquest. While this was certainly a period of expansion for Europeans, that expansion came at a great cost to other groups, including the native peoples of the Americas. In order to fully understand these global connections, you need to recognize the impact of trade, technology, religion and other factors.

Key technological innovations made the global connections of this period possible, both in terms of trade and exploration. These were, in particular, improvements involving navigation and ship-building. Improved maps were one factor in this process, but so too was the compass, the astrolabe, a device which was used to determine latitude, relying upon the stars to aid in navigation and improved sailing technology. The Portuguese developed the caravel, a small, highly navigable ship, and ideal for exploration, in the 15th century. The caravel quickly became widely used by various countries.

European Exploration

The explorations of European sailors and their patrons in the 15th century were not the result of a desire to discover new lands, but rather to discover better trade routes and spread European culture and the Christian religion. They were, at this time, particularly interested in South and East Asia, relatively untouched by earlier Christian missionaries and difficult to access for traders. The desire to convert new Christians was especially pressing for the Catholic Church in the face of the Protestant Reformation, which began at the very end of the 15th century.

On a Spanish-supported voyage, the Portuguese navigator, Christopher Columbus, discovered Cuba and the surrounding islands. He was attempting to find a new passage to East Asia. In the years following Columbus' initial voyage, various European countries sent expeditions west to explore the "new world". From the first reports, European monarchs and traders were interested in the goods this land had to offer. The Portuguese established a school of navigation, and efforts began to create colonies. Portugal and Spain controlled South American and Mesoamerica, while France and England began to colonize North America. Portugal also gained significant power in Africa, helping to increase its trade network, as it focused its explorations on African possibilities. By the end of the 15th century, the Portuguese had established direct sea trade with Africa and India.

Russia expanded its land holdings during this period. While sea passages were available to Russia, much of the year, ice blocked the harbors. Land expansion into Siberia was a higher priority for the Russian government at this time. Chinese explorers, supported by the government of the Ming Dynasty sent massive ships into the Indian Ocean. These ships brought back curiosities from India and Africa, including people, plants and animals, but the explorations soon ceased due to their high cost.

The Columbian Exchange

The Columbian Exchange refers to the trade in goods, people, and culture between the Americas and Europe following Columbus' 1492 voyage.

- The following came to the Americas from Africa, Asia and Europe: horses, pigs, chicken, cows, sugarcane, bananas, wheat and rice. Horses dramatically altered the culture of many Native American groups, while crops, particularly sugarcane, altered the land and eventually led to the import of massive numbers of slaves from Africa.

- The following came to Africa, Asia and Europe from the Americas: potatoes, tomatoes, tobacco, corn, chilies and cocoa. These foods, particularly corn and potatoes, dramatically increased food supply. Corn became a popular crop in Asia and Africa, while potatoes became common in much of Europe.

The Columbian Exchange cannot be discussed without considering the impact of disease on the Americas. Just as the Silk Road and other trade routes spread bubonic plague, the sailors from Europe brought illness with them. Some of these illnesses were typically relatively mild in Europe, as many people carried some amount of natural immunity. Others were more often still deadly in Europe, like smallpox. Smallpox and other illnesses, like influenza and measles, soon ravaged the Americas, wiping out as much as 90 percent of the population within just a few years.

In the Americas, the great empires of the Inca, in Peru, and the Aztecs, in modern-day Mexico fell to Spanish colonial forces and the diseases they carried. These formerly great empires were devastated by the conquest of the Americas and their fall was quick and brutal.

The Portuguese established substantial sugarcane plantations on the islands, but were left with a labor shortage. Spanish and Portuguese men had no interest in this physical labor, and the local population had already been destroyed by smallpox. Portuguese traders already had a solution to this labor shortage and Spain soon followed suit. African traders were willing to sell slaves, typically kidnapped from other regions of Africa, to be shipped across the Atlantic Ocean, a journey called the Middle Passage. Conditions were typically horrific on slave ships, and little better on the sugar plantations. Transports from Africa brought not only slaves, but also mosquitos, rice, and okra to the Americas. France, England and the Netherlands also held colonial holdings in the islands, with large-scale agricultural operations worked by slaves.

South America was rich in both gold and silver. Spain owned the gold mines, and the mined gold went directly into the Spanish royal treasury. Silver was more common, and with the support of the Portuguese, became a global trading currency. This provided both Europe and

Japan with more access to trade goods, while Asia and India took in a great deal of silver as the

primary exporters of goods.

Colonies in South America were the primary source of income for Western European

nations in this period. While England, France and Spain all took an interest in North America,

these colonies were smaller and less profitable. Fish, specifically cod, was the primary export

from this region. Several key terms are essential with regard to developing a thorough

understanding of trade during this era:

1. Triangle trade: The triangle consists of sugar, rum and fish moving from the Americas to

   Europe. In Europe, the goods are paid for with silver. The silver is used to buy slaves

   along the west coast of Africa.

2. Mercantilism: Mercantilism was the industry and regulation created by the trade in

   goods. Raw materials came to Europe and were made into manufactured goods and

   sold. Taxes and tariffs controlled the import and export of various goods.

In this newly global world, interactions also spread culture and religion. Islam continued

to spread; however, pushed no further into Europe and was, in the second half of the 15th

century, pushed out of Spain for good. Islam spread into Sub-Saharan Africa and further into

Southeast Asia during this time, with differences between Sunni and Shi'ite practices becoming

stronger. Sufism, an Islamic mystical tradition, was more common. Buddhism continued to

spread throughout Asia.

Christianity became more diverse, even as it spread. The Protestant Reformation had

divided the Catholic Church. In response, the Catholic Church initiated the Counter-Reformation.

This strongly Catholic viewpoint influenced the development of Christianity in Latin America.

The Protestant Reformation resulted in widespread religious discrimination, and eventually, many of the groups that came to North America were part of English Protestant groups, called Puritans.

- The Protestant Reformation began when, in 1517, Luther began to officially challenge the Catholic Church. While Luther had originally sought to reform the Church from within, quickly, a new Protestant Church formed, followed by a variety of other denominations. These churches rejected many traditional Catholic beliefs including the authority of the Pope, many of the sacraments, and the lack of vernacular translations of the Bible.

While many religions continued, new religions also developed during this period from different and varied traditions mingling and merging with one another, or religious syncretism. Examples of syncretism include:

- Vodun (voodoo) in the Caribbean which combined elements of Christianity and traditional African religions and was the direct result of slavery and forced conversion.
- Sikhism in India, combining elements of Hinduism and Islam.
- Cults of saints in Latin America, incorporating both Catholicism and elements of traditional religious practice.

The years between 1450 and 1750 are a time of great artistic and literary growth. In Europe, this is the period of the Renaissance or rebirth, with new vernacular literature, an interest in classical philosophy and learning, the development of new forms of theater and the rediscovery of classical art. Many of the greatest artists of European history date to this period. This interest in art and learning spread to Latin America as well. Elsewhere, the Bantu-speaking peoples of Africa built the city of Great Zimbabwe. Japan produced fine wood-block prints during this period, and miniatures were popular both in the Middle East and Europe. Noted authors include Shakespeare, Cervantes, while key works elsewhere in the world include the Epic of Sundiata, a ruler of the African nation of Mali, and the genre of Kabuki theater in Japan.

Social Interaction and Modes of Production

This was a period of change, throughout the world. While there were some consistencies, social change was widespread, both in the ruling elite and lower classes. New groups came to power, the impact of religious organizations changed and nearly all groups had to deal with a new level of interaction with outsiders. Agriculture changed, with the introduction of new foods and modes of production, as did the organization of labor. Population demographics shifted in the growing world.

New elites developed in many regions, replacing those formerly at the top of the social hierarchy. These elites held social, political and often, even religious power within their societies. They often had the ability to make and enforce laws, controlled the wealth of the state, and filled the majority of public and religious offices.

- **China**-The Qing Dynasty began in 1644 and lasted until the end of the Chinese Imperial era, in 1912. The Qing Dynasty was Manchurian, rather than Han Chinese. This minority gained and held power, but retained traditional practices within the Chinese court, including the bureaucracy of the imperial system, Neo-Confucianism, and the Mandate of Heaven. Merchants became wealthy, but still lacked social status.

- **Latin America**-European-born settlers were originally the most elite members of society in Latin America; however, soon the Creoles, or Latin American-born Europeans, held the greatest power. Below the Creoles were the Mestizos, or those of mixed European and native or African blood. Among the Mestizos, the more European blood, the higher the status. This was often determined less on ancestry and more on skin tone.

- **North America**-European settlers, particularly wealthy ones, retained power in French and English colonies. While there was a clear social hierarchy, there was little to no mingling between these settlers and native peoples. Those of African or Native American origin, or of mixed race, were not only lower in the social hierarchy, but often treated as sub-human.

- **Europe**-For the first time, business skill in the merchant or banking trades was a route to social and political power. Merchants could now not only become wealthy, but also quite powerful. Some even married into titles, while others, like the Medici family, created their own.

Traditional elites also retained power in some areas. In Europe, the noble families retained their wealth and power through this period in most regions. Key exceptions include the cities of Florence and Venice. In Japan, the daimyo retained significant social and political power, while the Zamindars held control of Moghul India.

While the elites changed in many areas, the majority of the population was far from the social elite. Most people were, as they had been in previous periods, peasants. They survived by working the land, or perhaps by working in a trade. They were, in modern terms, lower class, or at most, perhaps, lower middle class. While the status of tradesmen likely improved during this period, the status of peasants or agricultural labors declined. Coerced and forced labor became significantly more common in an increasingly commercialized agricultural world.

The work of the peasant classes intensified in many ways. In Russia, efforts to settle the rough and brutal Siberian frontier put Russian serfs at high physical risk. In India and China, the demand for fabrics, specifically cotton and silk, was high, leading to increasingly poor working conditions. In Europe, feudalism had come to an end, so peasants were now free to rent land and farm or to sell their goods at market. This is, however, before the industrial revolution, so labor should be considered on a small-scale, rather than in terms of large factories.

Forced and Coerced Labor

While even free peasants were limited in their options, given strict social hierarchies, financial limitations, and lack of access to education or opportunities for improvement, in many parts of the world, laborers were not free. They were coerced or forced to labor as slaves, indentured servants, or serfs. You should be aware of the following categories of coerced or forced labor.

- **Chattel slavery**-For most Americans, this is the most familiar form of coerced labor. Individuals were property, bought and sold, with no rights whatsoever. This form of slavery is, in this period, most common on sugarcane plantations in the Caribbean. Conditions on sugar plantations were so low that many lived only three years after arriving on the plantation. The vast majority of slaves were African. While chattel slavery is closely associated with the Caribbean and later, with the Southern United States, slaves were also exported into the Mediterranean Sea trading region and into the Indian Ocean trading communities.

- **Indentured servitude**-Indentured servitude was a temporary, contractual agreement. Young men and women often paid for their passage to the colonies by agreeing to servitude. After some number of years, their contract was paid off and they were free. They had significantly more rights than chattel slaves, but could not move elsewhere or stop working for the owner of the contract. Conditions varied for indentured servants, from quite good to very poor. They were not paid during the term of their contract, but were provided training, accommodation, and food.

- **The Hacienda System**-The Hacienda system was similar to a feudal system. The people working the land were typically forced to remain through a system of financial obligations. In this period, the workers were typically natives, rather than European immigrants.

- **The Mit'a**-The Inca had a system of required or forced public service, called mit'a. While under the Inca, the system was created with a great deal of flexibility, allowing men to contribute while still meeting the demands of their own family and land, the Spanish adopted the system, requiring that one-seventh of the male members of Inca communities provide labor in Spanish mines and other economic activities.

Demographic Changes and Shifting Roles

Populations changed significantly during this period, largely due to new interactions between people and regions. For some groups, these changes were positive, while for others, they were intensely and overwhelmingly negative. In some areas, demographic changes led to changing roles for people or changing gender roles.

In Europe, populations increased, thanks to an improved food supply. New crops, particularly the potato, supported population growth in Europe. While some people left Europe for the Americas, this change was relatively minimal. Wars continued to deplete the population throughout much of this period, including the Thirty Years' War in the 17th century.

As noted above, the native populations of the Americas were decimated, and in some areas, eliminated. While war and forced labor destroyed some portion of the population, the leading cause of death was disease, including influenza, measles and predominantly, smallpox.

Furthermore, forced labor in the mit'a system reduced the number of available men, while many European men in Latin America took native wives, leading to an even greater reduction in the population.

In Africa, slavery took a massive toll on the population. In particular, men were preferred as slaves and often taken. Students should be aware, in this case, that "taken" typically refers to kidnapping, the most common way in which traders acquired new slaves. This not only dramatically reduced the population, but altered gender roles within African society. Traditionally, these cultures had been patriarchal, with men holding most of the social power. As groups were reduced to largely women, social structures changed.

While we often paint this period as patriarchal, in broad terms, not all cultures relegated women to minimal roles in society. In Southeast Asia, women had a long tradition of running and working in the markets, selling goods and managing trade. This was a high-status occupation, and as the region entered international trade, women maintained their traditional role, gaining wealth and power. In marriage, women gained the wealth of their husband, rather than forfeiting their own. In these cultures, daughters were celebrated at birth, as they could bring wealth and honor to their families.

Social change meant new power for some groups, like the Manchurians in China and wealthy merchants. It meant less power for others, including chattel slaves and indentured servants. Food supplies became more stable, but disease, in some regions, more common. In broad terms, one can fairly say that the discovery of the Americas benefited Europeans, but caused great harm to the peoples of the Americas and Africa.

During this era, some governments continued, growing and expanding, some dissolved and new states were created. The great colonial empires began in this period, as various European nations controlled land in the Americas, Africa and Asia. Outside of Europe, the Chinese Empire, under the Qing Dynasty, expanded.

The Formation and Growth of Empire

There were substantial and growing empires in China, Russia, and Western Europe. The Ottoman Empire and Mughal Empire were both somewhat smaller, but still important during this period. Nearly all of these were marked by totalitarian governments, typically either with an imperial or monarchial government structure.

Absolutist governments, in which a single ruler held absolute power, were the most common form of government in this period, both in Western Europe and elsewhere. Rulers had the power to make and enforce laws, with no checks and balances or restrictions on their behavior. They controlled the budget, choices, and the presentation of the government, as well as international relations.

There is one distinct exception to the absolutist nature of government in the world during this time-Britain was a constitutional, rather than an absolutist monarchy. Established in 1689, during the Glorious Revolution, Britain's constitutional monarchy had limited powers and required the consent of parliament for many actions. At this time, the House of Lords and established nobility still held power, rather than the common people; however, there were limits on the power of the British monarch.

Rulers used a variety of tactics to legitimize their rule. They created an image of themselves as ruler, in a sense marketing themselves to ensure the loyalty of their people and the respect of other countries.

- The arts were one tool for political display. This included works of visual art, literature supporting the social hierarchy and massive architectural constructions. Both secular rulers and the Pope used art and architecture to legitimize power. Well-known examples include the paintings of the Sistine Chapel and the French palace at Versailles.

- Religion was also used to legitimize rule. In China, the emperor held a Mandate of Heaven allowing him to rule, while French kings ruled by divine right. Coronations were typically held in religious facilities, particularly in Christian countries.

In China, the Qing Dynasty expanded into Central Asia and Mongolia, as well as gaining control of Taiwan. Conquered peoples were largely allowed to retain their rulers, customs, and religion under Chinese rule. With sea trade becoming more prominent, the Qing allowed the Silk Road to fall into disuse. Pastoralism also became less common during this era, replaced by more stable and less mobile forms of farming. The Chinese empire was under the control of the emperor, who ruled with absolute power and the Mandate of Heaven.

Russia began to move into a position of prominence in the late 15th century, with the rule of Ivan the Great. Russia conquered lands to the East, South and West during this period. Expansion continued during the reigns of Peter the Great and later, in the 18th century, Catherine the Great. From the time of Peter the Great onward, Russia began to actively engage and interact with Western Europe, becoming a key player in the political activity in Europe. While modernization began under Peter, Catherine proclaimed Russia to be part of Europe and invited European immigrants. Russia was an absolute monarchy, and the institution of serfdom, a form of coerced labor, continued.

While the Byzantine Empire had been a great power in the previous era, it fell to the Muslim Ottoman Empire in the middle of the 15th century. The Ottoman Empire included North Africa, Southwest Asia, much of modern-day Turkey and large parts of Eastern Europe, almost to the border of the modern nation of Austria. The capital of the Ottoman Empire was Istanbul, formerly known as Constantinople. The Ottoman army was made up largely of Janissaries. Janissaries were trained from a young age. The Janissaries ere part of a system called devshirme and were recruited from Christian families. While the system was not voluntary, there was a great deal of opportunity for Janissaries and families, often, participated quite willingly.

Western European countries did not develop large land empires. These nations relied upon more distant sea empires, rather than land. England, France, Holland and Spain are all noted European colonial powers. All held colonies in various places, including the Caribbean. Natives and slaves were typically converted; however, Spain was the most prone to conversion by force of these. England and the Netherlands, both Protestant countries, were more tolerant. Spain also retained significantly more control over their colonies abroad than the other Western European powers. The Spanish monarchs held close power over their colonies, through Viceroys, while British and other colonies were typically managed by more independent local governments. Spain and Portugal also had lands in the Indian and Pacific Oceans.

As empires expanded, many nations were faced with new ethnic diversity. Groups had different customs, different religions, and often different ethnicities. Some governments, like the Manchurian Qing Dynasty, opted to support diversity and tolerance as they acquired land. Others were less tolerant of diversity, requiring, for instance, religious conversion. Some empires, like the Muslim Ottoman Empire, took a middle path. While Christians were not required to convert, they paid higher taxes and were required to provide some number of boys to serve the Ottoman emperor. The goals of all of these policies were to create stability, while exploiting the economic value of any minority populations.

New Governments of the Period

While many of the empires discussed above had their roots in earlier states and even earlier empires, a number of distinctly new governments developed during this period. These were, sometimes, entirely new, and in other places, a distinct and different continuation of past governments.

- Tokugawa Japan was an isolated state led by a military leader or shogun. Only a single trading vessel from Europe was allowed per year.
- Mughal India was a land empire, led by a Muslim ruler, with largely Hindu subjects. Mughal leaders lost power from 1750 onward, as the British gained control of India.
- The Netherlands were an economic power, focused on trade, particularly in Southeast Asia.

Conflict

There were a number of major conflicts during this period. These include competition for land, for trading rights, and for local control.

Trade rivalries concerned the rights to trade, access to the seas, and the ability to dock in ports. In the Caribbean, pirates threatened free trade, including ships sent out by various nations. Piracy was a significant problem for traders, as well as those traveling to Caribbean islands. The Omani Empire, located in East Africa, controlled a significant part of the Indian

Ocean basin from 1650 onward. This led to conflict with European traders, particularly since the Omani had successfully forced the Portuguese out of some parts of Africa.

State rivalries are conflicts between states. During this period, the most significant of these in Europe was the Thirty Years War. The Thirty Years War, from 1618-1648, involved all of the major European powers, but was mostly fought in modern-day Germany. The war was remarkably destructive and was among the longest continuous conflicts in history. Conflicts between Protestantism and Catholicism were central to this war, with the sides largely divided on the basis of religion. The Ottoman-Safavid War in the early 17th century was a conflict over land, as the two empires fought for control of Mesopotamia, including the city of Baghdad. This was a long-lasting conflict that had begun long before as the Ottomans sought to gain land from the Safavid Empire or Persians. Modern-day Iraq was lost to the Ottomans in this conflict.

Internal conflicts were also a challenge for many governments. These included:

- Peasant uprisings, often as the result of unfair treatment or food shortages.

- Religious conflicts, for instance, Protestants and Christians in France.

- Military uprisings, like the Samurai revolts in Japan.

Summary

- Trade networks grew in a new global market.
- The introduction of European settlers and illnesses destroyed the Inca and Aztec Empires and killed approximately 90 percent of the native population of the Americas; however, the impact on North America came somewhat later.
- Slavery grew significantly, with the majority of the slaves bought by plantation owners in the Caribbean. The slave trade formed one part of the Triangle Trade.
- Empires grew, particularly for European powers, but also for China and the Ottomans in this period.
- The Protestant Reformation altered the religious climate of Europe, and later, the Americas. Missionaries to other regions were less successful.

Period 5: 1750 CE to 1900 CE

The years between 1750 and 1900 CE are a time of revolution, both industrial and political. This period includes the American and French Revolutions, Napoleon's victories, and the key technological changes of the Industrial Revolution. This is also a time of significant imperial domination. People became increasingly mobile, thanks to improvements in technology, making it easier to travel long distances and helping to support the growing globalization of the world. Social reform also occurred during this period, as the lower classes gained new rights in some parts of the world.

The key concepts identified for Period 5, from 1750 to 1900 by the College Board are:

1. Global Integration and Industrialization
2. Imperialism and the Formation of the Nation-state
3. Nationalism, Revolution and Reform
4. Global Migration

You should note that there are four, rather than three key concepts in this period.

Industrialization was a slow process, rather than a violent revolution. This was a process based on technological innovation and one which grew as inventors and engineers built upon earlier work. Prior to the Industrial Revolution, there were relatively few consumer goods and goods were typically manufactured or produced in cottage industry, often the home or small workshops. Production of goods involved only minimal machinery, typically requiring a great deal of personal effort.

- For instance, producing cloth before the Industrial Revolution required the following: A farmer or herder raised a sheep, which were sheared for wool. The wool was cleaned and carded, or brushed smooth. The carded wool was then spun, by hand, using a drop spindle, to produce thread or yarn. This thread or yarn was then woven into cloth, using a loom worked by one or two weavers. Finally, the fabric was dyed to its final color.

With a growing global trading market, there was a high demand for more goods, different types of goods, and the means to move goods from place to place. As well, there was a significant need for improved mechanisms to acquire raw materials.

The Industrial Revolution did not come forth out of nothing. A number of factors had to be present in order for these changes to occur, including historical, social, cultural, geographic and commercial factors. The Industrial Revolution began in Europe, predominantly in England, so all of these factors should be considered with that in mind.

1. Geographically, Europe had easy access to the Atlantic, making it an ideal center for trade networks.
2. Coal, iron and timber were all accessible in England and the remainder of Europe.

3. The population of Europe had increased substantially, thanks to the introduction of new food stuffs, like the potato, from the Americas, as well as improved methods of food production.

4. More of the population now lived in urban areas, providing a workforce.

5. Trade had provided substantial capital.

6. Many areas of Europe had navigable rivers, providing both transportation and access to water for new industries.

Factory Production and Technological Innovation

The first step in the Industrial Revolution focused on an important and common consumer good—fabric. Fabric was traditionally labor intensive and costly to produce and, for the lower classes, often made at home, rather than bought. The mechanization of this process made fabric, and along with it, clothing, less expensive. New machines, like the spinning jenny, mass produced thread and cloth. While the first of these machines were still powered by hand, later, larger factories were built relying upon water-power, like water wheels, to power the machinery. Eventually, in America, the cotton gin was invented, cleaning the seeds from cotton far faster and more efficiently than humans could.

Inventors in Britain developed the steam engine in the 1760s. The steam engine produced power on demand, without easy access to a convenient source of flowing water, as required by water wheels. Factories could be located anywhere, including in cities and steam power was far more efficient than water power, dramatically increasing the rate of production. Steam engines, and later, the internal combustion engine, made accessing fossil fuels, like coal, both more practical and more necessary. While the first steam engines were put to use in industrial and mining settings, later steam engines found an even more important use.

Factory production continued to grow and develop, quickly spreading to the United States and continental Europe, before eventually moving into other parts of the world. This was a slow process sand some regions, even those with close contact with more industrialized areas, were slow to change. Unlike former cottage industry, factories had a large number of workers working in a single location to produce much larger quantities of goods. The organization of work had changed dramatically.

A second Industrial Revolution followed in the second half of the 19th century, with a number of new innovations. These included chemicals, electricity, and improved machinery capable of finer work than previously possible by machine.

In the early 19th century, the steam engine found a new home in two new forms of transportation: the steamboat, invented in America and the steam locomotive, or train, invented in Britain. These made it far easier to transport raw materials, manufactured goods and people than ever before. Eventually, streetcars and even subways were developed, moving people not only around the countryside, but through cities with ease.

These new innovations required a great deal of raw material. The steam engines ran on coal, while later internal combustion engines, not unlike those in our cars today, ran on petroleum, and later gasoline. While coal mining was critical to steam power, coal was not the only essential raw material. Areas rich in raw material exported raw materials and imported manufactured goods in their place. Raw materials ranged from fossil fuels to cotton to sugar and palm oil. Metals, wheat, sugar and even meat were also exported.

While some nations industrialized broadly, with industrialization spreading throughout the country, in others, industrialization divided the country, as in America. In the agricultural south, the demand for raw materials grew. For instance, while sugar plantations had been the primary importer of slaves in the early 18ᵗʰ century, after the industrialization of textile production, cotton plantations in the American South used a huge amount of slave labor as Southern agriculture focused on producing these raw materials for export. The north produced goods for export, rather than importing goods. Eventually, this led to not only conflicts over slavery, but also tariffs on imported goods. Following the victory of the north in the Civil War, legal and economic policies favoring industrialization prevailed. These were supported by the creation of an extensive rail network, with a coast-to-coast railway completed in 1869.

Some industries were placed near sources of raw materials. For instance, steel production required both coal and iron, so sites near sources of both were favored for steel production. Steel enabled new forms of construction that was relatively cheap, durable, and somewhat faster to build. Steel production was particularly strong in America.

While the Industrial Revolution brought new goods to the market and created new jobs in urban settings, it was damaging to the economies of agricultural countries. For instance, cotton had traditionally been a small-scale cottage industry in India. Now, it was far cheaper for Britain to import raw cotton and produce it in factories in Britain. The same happened in other agricultural economies.

An increase in manufactured goods led merchants to seek out new markets in which to sell their goods. These were not luxury goods, but rather basic items intended for regular use and a middle class market. Efforts to seek out new markets for goods even led to violence, as occurred when Britain sought to open up China as a potential import market in the 19ᵗʰ century. The French also hoped to open up the Chinese market. China preferred to remain relatively isolated; however, and had minimal interest in western goods. Spheres of influence were created within China allowing for trade, even as the government resisted. While China resisted, U.S. efforts to open Japan's trading borders were met very differently. Traditionally quite isolated, Japan embraced westernization and industrialization, becoming a successful exporter of factory-produced silk fabrics. Russia and Latin America, while exposed to industrialization and with the resources available, were slow to industrialize and many other countries lacked the financial resources necessary for industrialization. Africa failed to industrialize; however, key mining centers for gold and diamonds developed, particularly in South Africa, during this time.

Investment and Finance

The Industrial Revolution required capital or funds, in order to pay for factories, building projects, and development of major projects, like railways and steamboats. The relatively long history of trade for Britain and other European countries had already provided these nations with significant capital, both publicly and privately held. As discussed in earlier chapters, banking had developed in response to the needs of the trading community.

Banks, developed in Europe during the Renaissance, now offered loans to cover the cost of factories and other business ventures in a newly industrializing world. Banks were now a key part of the growing industrial complex, enabling both private and public business ventures to exist. Eventually, many nations standardized their currency against the gold standard, enabling the creation of logical exchange rates, so the value of one currency to another currency could be compared with ease.

A few other key parts of the modern financial world also developed during this period. These have continued, with some changes, into the modern day, but form a critical part of the world's financial organizations today.

- Insurance, for property and business ventures
- The concept of the limited liability corporation or LLC

- The stock market and publicly owned corporations, bought and sold in shares on the market

The first large multinational corporations also developed during the Industrial Revolution. The best-known of these are the Dutch East India and British East India Companies. By the middle of the 19th century, the British East India Company not only served a business function, but also a political one, controlling much of India. In the United States, the United States Fruit Corporation owned a large number of banana plantations in Central America, shipping produce to Europe and the United States.

Communication Technology

As discussed, steam engines paved the way for industrial machinery, locomotives and steam boats, making factory production and transportation possible. Communication also changed dramatically during the Industrial Revolution. This helped to support the growing globalization of industry, as messages could travel quickly from place to place. The telegraph was invented in 1840, crossed the Atlantic by the middle of the 1850s and reached around the world by 1900. This enabled messages to go from place to p lace through telegraph offices. Later in the 19th century, the telephone was developed, allowing for person-to-person communication.

Scientific Innovation

This is a period of significant scientific discovery. Chemists began working in earnest to learn more about the world around them and develop solutions to ongoing problems. The first chemical fertilizers and pesticides date to the 19th century, along with new fabric dyes and medications. New vaccines changed the experiences of many, as vaccinations for smallpox protected many from the disease. Eventually, anesthesia and a new understanding of germs made surgery and medical procedures safer than ever before. The recognition of water-borne illness led to safer, cleaner water supplies, and improved hygiene in the cities, including appropriate sewage systems.

At the end of this period, Charles Darwin recognized the process of evolution, publishing the Origin of Species. Darwinism provided explanations for many things recognized by the scientific community; however, it also led to social Darwinism, which applied Darwin's theory of the survival of the fittest to human groups and populations.

Industrialization and Social Change

Industrialization led to significant social change, altering the demographics of population, family structures and daily life. Farming required fewer laborers, as machines allowed fewer people to do the same amount of work. This reduced the work options for agricultural workers. Factories needed large amounts of labor and offered, in many cases, better wages. As workers moved into the cities, cities grew larger. This led to increased pollution, inadequate housing, and other problems connected with rapid growth.

Many families moved to the city to take industrial jobs. Early in the Industrial Revolution, women and children were often employed; however, later regulations provided labor protections for children and often reduced options for women. Children were often still employed in coal mines and agriculture, even after labor laws eliminated child labor in factories. Eventually, laws about school attendance ensured that children would be in school, rather than in the workplace.

With the growth of industrialization, the middle class grew. This population wasn't wealthy, but had some amount of discretionary income. They could afford schooling for their children, food for their table, ready-made clothing and even household goods. The middle class is closely connected to the social values of Victorian England, in particular.

Increasing pay created a new phenomenon in the west, one in which the wife or mother stayed home and cared for the home, without providing a distinct financial contribution. Work options for women decreased, with "women's work" limited to nursing, teaching, or clerical work, or work that could be done in the home, like taking in mending, needlework or laundry. Women were rarely allowed to keep working outside the home after marriage. In Japan, silk factories were primarily worked by young women, often in very poor conditions. These young women have left poetry and other works describing their experience working under male employers.

In areas untouched by the Industrial Revolution or those in which it did not take hold, there were relatively few changes to the social structures.

Art and literature of the west in the second half of the 19th century reflects this industrial world. Key things students should know include:

- Realism, including urban scenes and scenes of working life, was popular in painting and sculpture, but is also found in literature, for instance, the work of Charles Dickens.

- Impressionism portrayed the cities, but in a new light. The impressionists sought the beauty, rather than the grit.

- Cameras provided both a new artistic medium, and the ability to capture a true likeness.

This is the age of massive empires, including the empires of Western Europe, particularly Britain, and, to a lesser extent, Japan and the United States. These were transoceanic empires, spanning much of the globe. By 1900, Britain claimed 25 percent of the land in the world, from Australia to Canada. The Americas were no longer the focus of colonial efforts, as they had been in the past. Asia and Africa were the desirable land masses during this period, and control of these lands was the first priority for colonial powers. Significant European colonial powers include Britain, France, Germany and the Netherlands. While Spain and Portugal were colonial powers in the previous period, their influence faded dramatically during this one.

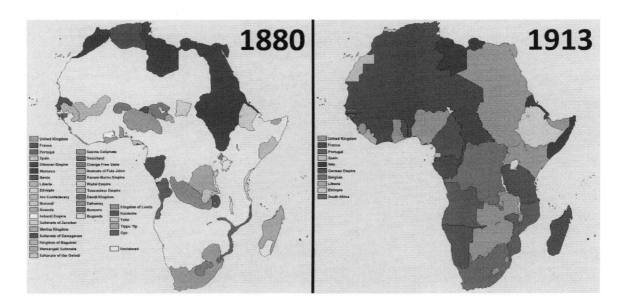

Figure 7 These maps illustrate the "Scramble for Africa" and the boundaries drawn by European colonial powers on that continent.[7]

The Growth of Empires

Why did empires during this period become larger and more successful than ever before? The answer is dependent on the technology of the Industrial Revolution. Steam-power made it easier to cross the seas than ever before, while railways allowed colonial powers

[7] By davidjl123 / Somebody500 (Own work) [CC BY-SA 4.0 (http://creativecommons.org/licenses/by-sa/4.0)], via Wikimedia Commons, accessed October 19, 2015.

improved access to land. Finally, and perhaps most importantly for the conquest of Africa, the machine gun offered the potential for extreme violence to suppress any possible rebellion.

This is also a period of intense nationalism, or a sense of pride in and devotion to one's own country, or the idea that one's country was the best. This sense of nationalism led countries to seek out the largest empire possible. Some of these were traditionally significant powers in Europe, including France, the Netherlands and Britain, while others were newer countries, just developing from disconnected former states, including Germany and Italy.

Figure 7 The map above illustrates all former British colonies.

The Growth of Colonial Power

In a number of cases, the growth of colonial power was a joint venture between both a government and a multinational corporation, like the British East India Company. Corporate interests often funded colonization projects, employed the soldiers and provided profits for the state, while the state approved the colonization. While nationalism was one factor encouraging colonialism, there was another as well—simple economics. Asia and Africa were rich in natural resources and raw materials, from gold and diamonds to rubber.

Early in the 19th century, the Dutch gained control of parts of Africa, followed by the French and Belgians. The British had a relatively small interest in Africa; however, this led to war between British and Dutch settlers in one instance. It is critical that you recognize the following about colonial governments, regardless of the colonial power. These are particularly true for Africa, as colonial efforts in Asia were less successful, largely as a result of relatively strong local governments.

- Europeans believed that their influence would benefit the people of the colonies. They brought learning, religion, and "civilization," considering colonization to be a burden particularly attached to white men. They did not consider the cultures they destroyed, violence, or other factors in their colonization of Africa and Asia.

- Social Darwinism supported the idea that conquering weaker lands and peoples was the right of the stronger and more powerful groups.

- Colonial powers split lands up amongst themselves with no regard for local borders, ethnic groups or religion. This has caused problems that continue today in countries like Nigeria. Africa was formally divided up at the Berlin Conference of 1884 and 1885.

- By the beginning of World War I, only Liberia and Ethiopia remained independent.

- Colonial governments varied, sometimes even within a single colony. Valuable regions were often more closely controlled by white, European governors, with locals more likely to retain some control in less valuable regions.

- Colonies are commonly separated into two types. White dominions existed where whites outnumbered native peoples, and the native population was often nearly or completely wiped out by disease or violence. Settler communities existed where there were communities of whites, but they remained a minority. Australia and the United States are examples of white dominions, while most African colonies were settler communities.

- White settlers typically took the most valuable land and used valuable resources. In many cases, white settlers lived a life of luxury while surrounded by poverty.

The local response to colonization varied. Some regions of Africa accepted white settlers and white control with limited violence, while rebellion was common in other areas. While many in the African ruling classes initially accepted European rule, some returned years later, with a European education, and actively rebelled against that rule.

In Asia, Europe held significantly less power. The primary colonial property in Asia was India, under the full control of the British Empire, with the extensive assistance of the British East India Company. The British East India Company held direct control of the territory until the middle of the 19th century. At that time, the government took more direct control; however, local forces were commonly used to maintain European power. The British also held Malaysia, Singapore and Hong Kong. Other small countries in the region were under the control of France.

In some cases, control in Asia was maintained and secured through treaties and other arrangements, rather than physical action. This is a form of economic imperialism, rather than white dominion or settler colonies. The strongest example of economic imperialism is found in China in this period, during and after the Opium Wars. Britain gained economic control through unequal treaties following the war, and other powers, including Russia and the United States took advantage of China's weaknesses.

The United States also pursued a policy of land acquisition during this period; however, some of the land was purchased, rather than taken by force. The Louisiana Purchase, in 1803, and the purchase of Alaska, in 1867 are examples of that, while the war with Mexico in 1840 led to the acquisition of Texas. At the end of this period, the Spanish-American War provided the United States with the Philippines and Puerto Rico. Properties in the Pacific, like Hawaii, helped to secure the role of the United States as a prominent naval power.

While Britain was quite well-established and the United States was gaining strength, even in the face of internal struggles, the discussion of empire requires that we include one very new empire, the German Empire. Germany united in 1871, having been, for centuries, a number of loosely linked relatively independent states. At the Berlin Conference, Germany claimed a number of colonial properties, including some in Africa and the South Pacific, improving its status in Europe. Students should keep Germany's interest in empire in mind as they progress into the next period of study.

While most imperial powers were western, Japan sought an empire of its own. From the mid-19th century onward, Japan, under the control of the western-influenced Meiji government, developed a strong, western-style military and quickly, in battles with China and Russia, gained land, including Korea. Japan was successful in building an empire and protecting itself from potential Russian incursion.

Not all empires grew during this era. In the face of growing European powers, the Muslim Ottoman Empire shrank, as it lost lands to European powers or to new, independent nations. It attempted to change, westernizing; however, the Empire met its formal end with World War I early in the 20th century. The Balkan nations gained new freedom, and Britain and France took control of parts of North Africa.

This is an age of great empires, providing powerful nations with ever more land and resources, to the detriment of local customs, cultures and populations.

This period is not only an era of empire building, but a time of significant internal change for a number of nations. As discussed in the previous section, this is a period of nationalism, or national pride for many countries. It was also the period, in Europe, of the Enlightenment, marked by a new interest in science, philosophy, thought and even, for the first time, human rights. As European culture spread through imperialism, the thought of the Enlightenment spread along with it.

Key Points in Political Enlightenment Philosophy

- Religion became less culturally important.

- John Locke developed the idea of natural rights.

- The social contract theory developed, suggesting that government exists and works because people agree to it.

- The notion of government checks and balances was developed by Montesquieu.

- Limited government was favored over totalitarian systems.

- Eventually, abolitionism, or the desire to abolish slavery, developed from Enlightenment ideas.

Revolution

Enlightenment thought and ideology supported a number of changes, not only in government, but in how people identified themselves. They developed ethnic or national identities, feeling joined to others by ties of religion, language or culture. This idea helped to create a spirit of nationalism, and often, a desire for change in government.

Near the end of the 18th century, two key revolutions occurred, both relying upon Enlightenment thinkers and ideas. All of these sought to create an Enlightenment government, specifically, a republic, without a king and with the people having a say in their government, approving it through a social contract.

In America, colonists sought their independence from British rule. After winning the Revolutionary War, the United States drafted documents based on Enlightenment theories, including the Declaration of Independence and Bill of Rights. A few years later, the French sought their own independence, albeit less successfully, from a long-term perspective. During the French Revolution, the revolutionary government produced the Declaration of the Rights of Man. The French Revolution resulted in a short-lived Republic, the Reign of Terror, and eventually a return to totalitarian rule under Napoleon Bonaparte. The Jamaica Letter contains a similar declaration of rights. These declarations of natural rights commonly left out several groups, including, in America, both slaves and women. Revolutions also occurred in some Latin American countries and Haiti, with similar goals. Haiti's revolution, led by slaves against a relatively small number of white colonists and overseers, was successful, but destroyed the economy. In Latin America, revolutions were led by the elite, who retained power, but were now free of Spanish or Portuguese rule.

Revolutions, including the American Revolution, did not provide all citizens with the natural rights or freedoms supported by the Enlightenment, but revolution stirred even in these groups. Groups of escaped slaves in America, Latin America, and the Caribbean Islands formed Maroon Societies. These ranged from small, short-lived communities to powerful larger communities numbering thousands of individuals. They formed an essential resistance against slavery.

The Maroon Societies and Haitian Revolution are not the only examples of a revolution led by an oppressed group against an oppressor. A number of countries experienced revolt and revolution of local groups against a colonial power. In India, Britain suppressed the Indian Revolt of 1857, while in China, the Boxer Rebellion challenged European authority and economic access. While some of these rebellions were largely political, others were much less so and were driven by religious or other motivations. The 19th century Taiping Rebellion was led by Hong Xiuquan, leading to civil war in China, largely based on the leader's religious visions. In the United States, the Ghost Dance movement supported resistance against white settlement. In some cases, imperial powers responded to rebellion, either through reform or violence.

Eventually, the changing political ideology throughout Europe and other parts of the world led to the development of a new array of political ideas, including socialism and communism. Within some countries, these movements helped to support various reforms, including workers' rights.

The Political Impact of Industrialization

Industrialization changed the boundaries, borders and face of Europe. The small villages became smaller, as fewer people were needed to work in agriculture and industry and manufacturing moved to the cities. Many people moved to the cities, relatively rapidly. Cities were not designed or constructed to manage populations of this scale, leading to a number of significant social difficulties, including:

- Overcrowding

- Poor housing

- Dangerous work conditions

- Lack of adequate access to water

- Inadequate sanitation, including sewage systems

- Spread of infectious disease

Conditions in the cities contributed to a number of movements among the lower classes for additional rights and protections. These movement sought both additional political control for the lower classes, the urban working poor, and additional protections, like the ability to strike and fair labor laws. Labor unions formed during the period between 1820 and 1840, but were still illegal through most of Europe. By the late 1840s, the interest in Marxism spread, advocating the overthrow of the upper classes by the workers. In 1848, revolutions sprang up throughout Europe; however, many were short-lived.

Some improvements were made in cities throughout Europe during the middle of the 19th century, particularly with regard to water supplies and sanitation. Public housing projects were built in some cities, and the German Empire introduced unemployment payments and social security programs. Even as technology improved, famine struck Europe, with the Irish potato blight in the middle of the 19th century decimating the Irish population, both through starvation and emigration. Eventually the Irish potato famine led to improved social welfare programs to assist the poor.

While the first movements were focused on working men, over the course of the 19th century, more and more women began to demand rights, including the right to vote, or suffrage. Several key moments in the women's rights movement in the west are:

- Mary Wollstonecraft's *A Vindication of the Rights of Women*
- The Seneca Falls Conference in Seneca Falls, NY in 1848

You should be aware that women in the U.S. and Britain did not gain the right to vote until after World War I.

When we speak of global migration in this period, we mean, by and large, migrations from Europe, Asia and Africa to the Americas. These include both voluntary migration and forced migration.

People chose to immigrate to the United States and other places in the Americas for a number of reasons, commonly called push/pull factors. Push factors are reasons to leave a place, while pull factors are reasons the new location is appealing. The majority of immigrants, but certainly not all, were young men looking for opportunity.

- Common push factors include a lack of available jobs, religious discrimination, a lack of economic opportunity or poor environmental conditions. An increase in population was also a push factor in many regions, as it limited access to jobs and opportunity.

- Pull factors are a good job market, access to land and resources, freedom of speech and religion, and improved environmental or climatological conditions. Areas with lower populations were more appealing as they offered more opportunities.

Immigrants, particularly manual laborers, saved to pay for their passage, often with the assistance of family. In some cases, immigrants signed indentured servitude contract. This was, in the 19th century, especially common for immigrants from Southeast Asia; however, in some cases, indentured servitude is a form of coerced migration or forced migration. While some immigrants were manual laborers, many others were skilled professionals, choosing to move for better opportunities in the Americas. Other individuals opted for temporary migrations, working away from home for a better income, without permanently leaving their homes. Eventually, countries began to attempt to regulate immigration, using laws and limits to impact the number of immigrants arriving from different countries.

Immigrants formed communities in their new countries, often maintaining traditional language, religion and culture. These communities often provided comfort and support for new immigrants and many remained within their communities. The Chinese communities in many big cities, particularly on the West Coast of the United States are an excellent example of these enclaves.

As large numbers of men left their homes to migrate in search of better opportunities, women frequently remained behind. In some cases, men sent for their families some years later, after getting work or establishing a farm. The women who remained frequently took on new social and economic roles in their families.

Summary

- The Industrial Revolution changed the demographics and daily life throughout significant parts of the world.
- The steam engine, locomotive, steam boat, and internal combustion engine are all critical inventions of the Industrial Revolution.
- European powers, in particular, sought to acquire land and form empires. Land in Africa was most commonly claimed through violence, while land in Asia was often acquired through unequal treaties.
- Revolutions in Latin America, France and the United States relied upon Enlightenment philosophy for ideas about natural rights and government.
- Large numbers of people migrated from Asia, Europe and Africa to the Americas.

While this period is almost certainly more familiar to you, it is still a time of great change, both in terms of technology and politics. This unit covers the 20th century through the modern-day, including changing gender roles, economies, technology and both world wars. The global interactions noted in previous periods become more important as travel and communication becomes progressively more accessible.

The key concepts identified for period 6 by the College Board are as follows:

1. Science and the Environment

2. Global Conflicts and Consequences

3. Global Economy, Society and Culture

The years since 1900 have seen immense changes in science and technology. Early in this period, these changes are a continuation of work begun in the 1800s, including electricity and the telephone. Later innovations move further away from the original roots of technology, the steam engine and combustion engine. Below, you will find an introduction to key technological innovations.

Electricity

Today, electricity powers our homes, businesses, schools, and sometimes, even our cars. At the turn of the 20th century, electricity was still quite uncommon, with only the wealthiest having access to it. Even those who could access electricity often chose not to, frightened of this new technology. Electricity gradually became more common and more accessible. With electricity, lights allowed factories to work through the night and people could continue their activities after dark. Appliances, like the refrigerator and radio, became common in western countries, but electricity was slower to reach Asia and Africa. Today, some parts of Africa remain without electricity. Electricity can be generated in a variety of different ways; however, fossil fuels are still commonly used. Nuclear power is common in some, but not many, areas to provide power and is controversial after serious nuclear incidents in the Soviet Union in 1986 and Japan in 2011. Solar and wind power offer more environmentally-friendly options to generate electricity for homes and businesses.

Communication

Invented in 1876, the telephone provided the first option for easy, immediate long-distance communication without a trained professional. Through the early 20th century, telephones were used primarily by the wealthy, in North America, Europe, Australia and Japan.

By the 1920s, the telephone became more common. As telephones became more common and accessible, the telegram became less necessary or practical. Telephone technology remained relatively stable until the 1980s, when cellular phones became common. Today, cellular phones have replaced land-based phone lines for many people.

Radio and television are also a means of communication; however, they are one-way, rather than two-way, like the telephone. Radios became common after World War I, and were in many homes during the 1920s in the more developed world. The radio brought news, information, and entertainment into living rooms in Europe, the United States and other more-developed countries. Throughout World War II, the radio was a key source of daily news. Television was invented in the middle of the 20th century, and had become quite popular by the 1960s in the United States, and somewhat later elsewhere.

Computers today play a key role in communication technology. The first computer was built in 1940 and they were not accessible to the public until the early 1980s. By the early 1990s, people had begun to use networks to talk with other computers, marking the beginning of the internet. Today, internet access is widely available around the world, even in areas sometimes lacking other services.

Transportation

The railways revolutionized the world in the 19th century, along with the steam boat and steam-powered ship. Trains remained important through much of the 20th century in some areas; however, they were joined by the automobile, powered by an internal combustion engine. Cars became progressively more common in more-developed parts of the world, enabling people to travel longer distances with ease. This allowed travel, but also created larger suburbs around cities and made it easier to transport goods, including perishable goods. The popularity of the automobile has significantly contributed to environmental damage, including global warming. Later, air travel made it possible to cross the ocean in a matter of hours rather than weeks. In light of the next chapter, on conflicts, it is critical to note that these same innovations made it possible to move troops rapidly from place to place.

Science

Changing technology has been accompanied by a changing understanding of science, from how we perceive our world to medical science. Scientific discoveries have led to longer lives, more devastating weapons, and a better quality of life, including a more stable and adequate food supply.

The scientific method was well-established and many scientists in the 19th century were making remarkable discoveries. Late in the 19th century, Darwin recognized the importance of evolution. Key scientific theories and realizations in the 20th century include:

- Einstein's Theory of Relativity, explaining the variable nature of the universe

- The Big Bang Theory, explaining the origin of the universe

- Quantum Mechanics, the study of the world at a nanoscopic level

- The science of psychology, the study of the operation of the human brain

Advancements in chemistry created the Green Revolution. The Green Revolution dramatically changed the food supply, increasing access to adequate food around the world. Hybridization has particularly improved food supplies in Asia and Southeast Asia, but has provided relatively little relief for Africa. While fertilizers and pesticides were part of the earlier Green Revolution, today, the Green Revolution also includes genetically modified plant crops.

Medical science has taken immense leaps and bounds in the years since 1900. While sanitation and anesthesia were key improvements in medicine in the 19th century, the 20th century saw the invention of antibiotics, improvements in sterilization techniques, and additional vaccine development. Vaccines eliminated many common and dangerous illnesses. New surgical procedures and cancer treatments extended life and provided treatment options in a wide variety of situations. While medical options are widely available in wealthier countries, lower life expectancy is still a significant problem in less-developed countries, particularly in Africa.

Improved medical technology has reduced the risk of epidemics, but they have not been eliminated. Diseases traditionally associated with poverty remain a problem, particularly in Africa, including malaria, tuberculosis, and dysentery. Inadequate clean water and sanitation continues to spread disease. Modern epidemics, including HIV and Ebola disease, are impacting impoverished areas of Africa most strongly. Diseases have impacted the world population significantly. In 1918, just as World War I ended, as many as 20 million people died in the Spanish Flu epidemic. Since its discovery, approximately 25 million people have died of HIV/AIDS. By the early 21st century, the majority of deaths from HIV/AIDS occurred in Africa. Some diseases, typically linked to either lifestyle or age, became more common, particularly in the west. These include diabetes, heart disease and many types of cancer.

Population

With better food supplies, medicine, reduced infant mortality and a longer life span, the population continued to grow substantially through the 20th century. The highest population concentrations exist in East and Southeast Asia, primarily China and India; however, the population of China has experienced negative growth after restrictive population policies.

Population growth is relatively low in the west, but remains high in less-developed nations. Access to contraception has dramatically lowered the birth rate in the west, as women can choose how many children to have and plan for those children. In China, a restrictive one-child policy limited population growth, but brought challenges in terms of gender disparity and an adequate young workforce. In India, restrictive policies have failed to reduce growth. In Africa, birth rates remain high and many women lack access to contraceptives.

Government policies encouraging or discouraging births are one factor in population, but war and famine have also impacted population significantly during the 20th century. New wartime technologies and tactics led to more deaths than ever before in war. In World War I, trench warfare, mustard gas and the machine gun contributed to high fatalities, while the atom bomb, tank, and aircraft played a role in the high fatalities in World War II.

- In World War I, as many as eight million soldiers and 12 million civilians died.
- In the Russian Civil War, approximately 20 million people died.
- Approximately 60 million people died in World War II, including victims of the Holocaust, soldiers, and civilians.

Civilian casualties are often the result of widespread bombing, as in Dresden, Hiroshima and Nagasaki during World War II; however, other urban populations were devastated by ground fighting, like Nanjing in the early 1930s.

Famine also impacted civilian populations during and after war, with many of the deaths in the Russian Civil War attributed to famine. Relief efforts from the United States prevented widespread famine in Europe after World War II. Famine can be the result of the destruction of war, but can also be the result of intentional manipulation of the food supply. In the Soviet Union in the 1930s, Stalin issued orders that created a famine in the Ukraine, commonly called the Holodomor. This forced starvation led to as many as 13 million deaths. Following the Communist Revolution in China, Mao's government engineered a famine responsible for up to 20 million dead. These famines were not the result of a poor harvest, a potato blight or destruction of war, but rather the manipulation of food supplies to keep food away from particular populations.

Pollution

A growing population and industrial development have led to widespread pollution. Beginning in the 1970s, in the west, efforts were made to better manage wastewater and other forms of industrial pollution; however, these continued in other parts of the world. Industry is not solely responsible for pollution. The individual carbon footprint, or resources used daily, is quite high in the west, particularly the United States. The use of cars, wasteful use of electricity and other resources and typical American lifestyle contribute to this. European countries have been at the forefront for reducing resource usage, while less-developed countries use less as there is less opportunity to do so. Today, widespread pollution has led to an increase in global temperatures.

In order to fully understand the nature of the global conflicts and consequences of the 20th and 21st century, you need to recognize the world as it stood in the year 1900. Take just a moment to review the world order prior to World War I.

- European countries had divided up Africa and held control over parts of Asia. They vied for power amongst themselves.

- The young German Empire was growing in strength during this time.

- Japan had developed a strong, westernized government.

- The United States was gaining political strength and power.

- Land-based empires, including the Ottoman, Russian and Qing were weakening.

World War I

A number of factors led to the beginning of World War I, many discussed in the previous chapter. This war was the eventual result of the imperialism, nationalism and technological growth of the 19th century. By the end of the 19th century, lands had been claimed, and there was little room left to expand, making imperialism and the competition that accompanied it increasingly problematic. Nationalist ideologies and a growing rivalry between Britain and Germany also contributed. While the beginning of the war is marked by the assassination of Archduke Franz Ferdinand in Sarajevo on June 28, 1914, widespread ethnic tensions were already present, as groups sought more independence from larger imperial powers, like Austria-Hungary. The Industrial Revolution had led to the production of more dangerous weapons than ever before, including machine guns.

Various alliances existed among the powers in Europe early in the 20th century. Understanding these alliances is essential to thoroughly understanding the conditions that led to World War I. You should recognize these as competing alliances and realize that it is these alliances that shaped the war.

- The Triple Entente consisted of Russia, England and France.

- The Triple Alliance included Germany, Italy and Austria-Hungary.

These alliances later changed, both in name and composition. The Triple Entente is commonly referred to as the Allies, while the Triple Alliance becomes the Central Powers. Italy declared neutrality early on in the war, but eventually entered the war with the Allies, and Germany allied itself with the Ottoman Empire. Be conscientious not to confuse the Triple Alliance and the Allies!

All of these factors contributed to tensions in Europe in 1914. When Archduke Franz Ferdinand, the heir to the empire of Austria-Hungary was assassinated by a Serbian separatist in Bosnia, tensions erupted. Declarations of war came soon after, in rapid succession. The Archduke's assassination took place on June 28 and by August 7, most of Europe was at war. The Germans planned to quickly take France, a plan known as the Schlieffen Plan; however, this failed. The Belgians resisted, limiting German movement and the Russians moved more rapidly than expected. The Germans were, unexpectedly, forced to fight a war on two fronts. The Russians pushed westward out of Russia and into East Prussia, while the battle for France took place in Belgium. By early September, the failure of the Schlieffen Plan became clear. Nations around the world rapidly became involved. Japan allied itself with the Allies, while the Ottoman Empire sympathized with the Central Powers. While fighting continued on two fronts in Europe, battles also broke out in Africa and Asia. Troops were called in from around the world, including forces from Canada and Australia.

By November 1914, Britain and France had declared war on the Ottoman Empire, Russia had

declared war on Serbia, and assorted other nations had stepped into the conflict in various

ways. Battles continue on multiple fronts into 1915, including Gallipoli, where the British

attempted and failed to reach the Ottoman capitol of Constantinople. In May 1915, the

Germans sunk a British passenger ship, the Lusitania, drawing significant American sympathy.

The Americans involved themselves diplomatically, but did not offer military support until, in

February 1917, the Germans resumed active submarine warfare and had taken action to try to

ally Mexico against not only the Allies, but also the United States. In June 1917, the first

American troops reached Europe.

The involvement of fresh, well-armed and healthy American troops changed the war, and

changed it relatively rapidly. While there had been no clear winner just months before, by early

1918, U.S. President Woodrow Wilson outlined Fourteen Points, envisioning terms to end the

war. The war came to an end on November 11, 1918, with an armistice. The final peace

settlement, the Treaty of Versailles would follow some time later. Amongst the terms of that

treaty was the creation of a League of Nations, much like the modern United Nations.

Unfortunately, that organization lacked the resources necessary to prevent war in the future.

The Treaty of Versailles sat forth harsh peace terms for the aggressors, particularly

Germany. Germany owed reparations payments to France, Belgium and other European powers

and its abilities to rebuild were limited. These conditions are critical for the eventual

development of the Nazi state and beginning of World War II.

The Russian Revolution and Formation of the Soviet Union

During the last years of World War I, after Russia had made its peace with Germany in an

unequal treaty, Russia experienced its own civil war, the Russian Revolution. Bolshevik or communist forces, called the Red Army, opposed Tsarist forces, or the White Army. The war was brutal, and eventually, the soviets, or workers councils of the Bolsheviks, prevailed. Eventually, Vladimir Lenin gained control of the newly created Soviet Union. Lenin died in 1924, and after a few years of conflict, Josef Stalin took control of the communist party. He implemented modernization plans, called Five Year Plans, focused on heavy industry. He would retain control until his death in 1953, expanding his control to extend through Eastern Europe, and ruling with an iron fist. Any rebellion was quickly eliminated, either through murder, planned starvation, or prison camps.

The Years between the Wars

The years directly after World War I were a time of rebuilding for much of the world. Germany lost its colonial properties in the war; however, France and England gained lands that had been under the control of Germany and the Ottoman Empire, defeated in World War I. Battles had been fought in modern-day Israel, Turkey, all over Europe and in many parts of Africa. Nonetheless, the 1920s are a time associated with relative financial success for many countries, with development and with progress, until the Great Depression, beginning with the stock market crash of 1929. This Depression was global, affecting much of the world. As stocks fell, fortunes were lost, and along with them, jobs. Most Americans are aware of conditions in the United States during the Depression, but this Depression also dramatically impacted Germany, triggering a total devaluing of German currency. The Germans could not afford to pay reparations ordered by the Treaty of Versailles and resentment was growing.

In Germany, during the Depression, resentment grew in a small political party. This political party would become, in the near future, the National Socialist or Nazi Party. While he did not found the party, within just a few years, a World War I veteran named Adolf Hitler, would come to lead it. Hitler was a persuasive and skilled speaker, and remarkably charismatic. He soon had

a close circle of followers in the Nazi party. While the party began in the 1920s, early attempts

at gaining power in Germany were unsuccessful and Hitler was even imprisoned, during which

time he wrote *Mein Kampf*. By 1930, the Nazi Party held a majority in Germany's parliament and

by February 1933, Hitler is fully in control of the German state. Following a fire, almost certainly

set by the Nazis, Hitler and his party secured power over Germany. In Italy and Japan, changes

to the government and economic systems occurred as well, as both embraced fascism, an

authoritarian form of nationalism. Here, you should remember that World War II didn't entirely

begin with Germany. In the early 1930s, both Japan and Italy invaded other countries. Japan

invaded Manchuria in 1931 and China in 1937. Spain also embraced fascism, leading to a civil

war. Fascism finally ended in Spain in the 1970s. Fascism was also adopted in some parts of Latin

America.

World War II

The history of World War II requires that you understand both the war itself, and also

the Holocaust, or mass murder of the Jews, Roma and other groups by the Nazi party. Hitler's

anti-Semitism was clear early in his personal history and was expressed politically from an early

stage, but legislation took somewhat longer, with the Nuremburg Laws, defining who was a Jew

and restricting the movement, work and relationships of Jewish people enacted in 1935. By

1938, Hitler had re-armed the German people and was in violation of the Treaty of Versailles. In

March, Hitler gained control of Austria, with the voluntary cooperation of the Austrian

government. Nonetheless, other European countries, including Britain and France, wanted to

avoid war, even giving Hitler a German-speaking portion of Czechoslovakia, the Sudetenland in

November 1938. November 1938 is also the first clear act of organized, government-mandated, physical violence against the Jews, with Kristallnacht, when Jewish businesses were looted and destroyed and many Jewish men arrested.

Germany's aggressive actions continued, and with the German invasion of Poland, war officially began. This brought an end to the European policy of appeasement. World War II began in Europe on September 1, 1939.

- The Allies included England, France and Poland. Later, other Western European nations, the Soviet Union and the United States would join the Allies, but early in the war, the Soviets had a non-aggression pact with Germany.
- The Axis included Germany, Italy and Japan.

By the middle of 1940, Germany had occupied much of Western Europe, including Luxembourg, Poland, Austria and France. Germany relied upon the *blitzkrieg* or lightning war strategy. This began with an air bombing, followed by tanks, quite quickly. Foot soldiers only entered to clean up any remaining resistance. This strategy was remarkably effective. In June 1941, the Germans invaded the Soviet Union, and the Soviets entered the war formally, on the side of the Allies. The Italians aggressively pursued control of North Africa, Greece and other regions. At the same time, Japan expanded its control of the Pacific.

On December 7, 1941, the Japanese bombed the U.S. naval base at Pearl Harbor in Hawaii. With this act of direct aggression, the United States entered World War II. War continued; however, the Allies made significant gains with the resources of the United States. On June 6, 1944, commonly called D-Day, huge numbers of American troops landed on the beach at Normandy. American troops pushed into Germany from the West and Soviet troops from the East. In May 1945, Germany surrendered and the European front was won. The war in the Pacific continued until August 1945. On August 6, 1945, the United States dropped an atomic bomb on Hiroshima, followed by another on the city of Nagasaki on August 9. The Allies accepted the formal surrender of Japan on September 2, 1945.

The German actions associated with the Holocaust occur concurrently with those of World War II. After gaining control of Poland in 1939, Germany established ghettos and forced the Jews to move into these ghettos. Initially, they were open, with people free to come and go, but not long after, they were closed, confining huge numbers to a very small space. In these conditions, disease, including typhus, and starvation were inevitable. Large scale killings followed, first by killing squads, called *Einsatzgruppen*, and later by the first death camps, including Chelmno, Belzec and Treblinka. These camps were replaced by Auschwitz-Birkenau. While there were concentration camps throughout German-controlled lands, these camps were designed primarily to eliminate as many people as possible, as rapidly as possible. In total, scholars estimate around 10 million people were killed in the Holocaust, including six million Jews.

After World War II ended, the Allies were left to reassemble a devastated world. Several key events occurred during the years immediately following the war.

- The United Nations was created, with far broader powers than the former League of Nations. The goal of the United Nations was to prevent atrocities and global war from occurring again.
- The state of Israel was created to provide a homeland for displaced Jews.
- Tensions between the Soviet Union and the west, particularly the United States, grew.

The End of Colonialism

Powerful transregional and transoceanic empires lost colonies, either through a process of negotiation or armed rebellion beginning in the early and middle part of the 20th century and

118

continuing through the second half of the 20th century. India and the Gold Coast negotiated independence from Britain peacefully, while the French lost Algeria and Vietnam to armed revolts among the local people. In India, Mahatma Gandhi promoted non-violence and peaceful solutions, seeking a unified and independent India. While India became independent in 1947, it was not unified. The Partition of India divided India into three nations; India, Pakistan and Bangladesh. While Britain and France gained colonial holdings after World War I, within the first decades after World War II, nearly all former colonial lands were granted independence, with the support of the United Nations. Some countries retained close relations with the colonial power, particularly white dominions like Canada and Australia. Many others sought to distance themselves from colonial history, including countries in Africa, some of which, like Nigeria, continue to struggle with the remnants of colonialism.

The Cold War

The Cold War began almost immediately after World War II and lasted until the collapse of the Soviet Bloc in 1989. Near the end of World War II, the Allies met at the Yalta Conference. It was agreed that the Soviet Union would take control of Eastern Europe, but with the promise of self-determination. During this conference, the U.S. gained political control of Japan and Korea was split into North and South, as it is today. This promise was not kept and communist regimes were put into place throughout Eastern Europe. While the Cold War did not include physical battles, the Soviets and Americans fought for control of land, to limit one another's power and to have bigger and more dangerous armaments than the other. Throughout this, western powers opted for containment, trying to avoid the spread of communism.

Key events in the Cold War include:

- The Soviet blockade of West Berlin. West Berlin was in the hands of the Western Allies; however, it was within Soviet-controlled territory. When the Soviets stopped allowing Allied vehicles through their lands, the Allies supplied West Berlin by dropping supplies from the air.

- The U.S. implemented the Marshall Plan to fund and rebuild Western Europe and Japan. By the early 1950s, these countries were all thriving. The Soviets were less successful.

- In 1949, the U.S. and Western European countries formed the North Atlantic Treaty Organization or NATO. In response, the Soviets and Eastern Bloc created the Warsaw Pact. These organizations were intended for defense, not trade or diplomacy.

- In 1950, North Korea invaded South Korea. The UN responded, sending troops led by the United States. Fighting lasted for three years and boundaries were eventually re-established. The Vietnam War occurred for similar reasons; however, there was a clear communist victory in Vietnam in 1975.

- In 1961, the Soviets built the Berlin Wall.

- In 1962, the Soviets placed missiles aimed at the United States in communist Cuba. This led to the Cuban Missile Crisis and nearly to all-out war.

- In 1989, the Berlin Wall fell, torn down by anticommunist groups in East Berlin. The Eastern Bloc and Soviet Union collapsed soon after, ending the Cold War. During the course of the early 1990s, most Eastern European countries established democratic governments. Today, it should be noted, there are growing concerns about the government of the Russian Federation, led by Vladimir Putin.

While the Cold War never turned into a violent, global war like World War II, it was expensive, tense and left a legacy of nuclear weapons.

Revolution in China

The Qing Dynasty was overthrown in 1911, leading to a relatively short-lived democratic government, under the leadership of Sun Yat-Sen. Following the death of Sun in 1925, the government was controlled by Chiang Kai-Shek. Strongly opposed to communist factions in the Chinese government, small scale battles broke out amongst communists and nationalists. Japan invaded in 1937, suspending the civil war during World War II. Following the end of World War II, the Civil War resumed, this time at a much greater scale than previously. In 1949, the communist party, led by Mao Zedong was victorious.

Immediately, Mao's government initiated sweeping changes in Chinese government and agriculture. Many of these were unsuccessful. After famine in the late 1950s, the Cultural Revolution led to the deaths and re-education of those who sympathized with the capitalist west. While China and the Soviet Union were the two largest communist states, they were not allied with one another. Gradual economic changes have lessened some controls within China; however, the state remains quite authoritarian.

Changes in the Middle East

Many of the conflicts in the modern world are centered on the Middle East. In order to understand these conflicts, you do need to learn a bit more about the history of the Middle East after World War II.

The conflict between Israelis and Palestinians is the direct result of the creation of Israel by the United Nations following World War II. In order to create Israel, the UN displaced a large number of people, pushing them out of their homes and limiting their access to religious sites. The conflict in this region, over these lands, has been ongoing since the creation of Israel, with significant periods of escalating violence.

In Iran, the 1979 revolution replaced a pro-Western government with a religious theocracy, led by a religious leader, the Supreme Leader or Ayatollah. The new Iranian government rejected western values and culture, implementing strict religious law. This new religious fundamentalism in Islam spread, eventually leading to the creation of Islamic terrorist organizations, including Al-Qaeda, responsible for the September 11, 2001 attack on the United States.

Conflicts and Culture

The global conflicts of the 20th and 21st century have influenced our understanding and awareness of culture in a variety of ways. The art of the German Expressionists in the 1920s revealed a growing fear of the Nazi party, while Pablo Picasso's *Guernica* illustrated the horrors of war. Today, books, movies and video games continue to embrace the history of war, as people play first-person shooters or sit down to read the recent bestseller, *Monument Men*.

Economy and Society

Culture, society and economics has, like conflict and technology, shaped the modern world. You should be aware of key trends and how they impacted the function of various countries around the world.

Economics

Economics has, as it did in earlier periods, played a key role in shaping historical events and actions. Governments took different approaches to economics during the course of the 20th and early 21st centuries. Below, you'll find summaries of the changing economic responses of government in different nations.

In the United States at the beginning of the 20th century, the government played little role in economic development or control. With the election of Franklin Delano Roosevelt and the introduction of the New Deal, this changed. The New Deal worked to stabilize banks, but also initiated large-scale government projects to put Americans back to work, from building national parks to working on highways to writing books about American attractions and history. American approaches to economics have varied since; however, these have included the creation of Social Security, Medicare and Medicaid, while still supporting a strong free market economy.

In communist states, the government controlled means of production and all economic ventures. This was often less successful than hoped. In the Soviet Union, the Five Year Plans did result in rapid industrialization; however, the quality of life of the population did not increase. In China, the Great Leap Forward was an utter failure. While the Soviet Union has collapsed, China has become an economic power by loosening restrictions on the market economy.

Many countries rely upon government investment and involvement to encourage economic prosperity. In China, this has been the introduction of special economic zones, while in other parts of the world, it consists of incentives to encourage exports.

Global Organizations

A number of global organizations exist to support interconnectedness and cooperation in the modern world. These began with the post-World War I League of Nations, but today include the United Nations, the economic G7, the International Criminal Court, the Olympic Committee and a number of other groups. These groups each serve a different function.

- The UN and International Criminal Court provide legal protections and the means to enforce them, while supporting cooperation between nations.

- The International Monetary Fund, World Bank and G7 are all economic organizations.

- The World Health Organization responds to health crises.

- UNICEF, The Red Cross, and Doctors without Borders are all examples of humanitarian organizations that respond to various humanitarian needs, for instance, working in refugee camps.

- Trade agreements and organizations exist to regulate international trade, as well as the business of multinational corporations. NAFTA-the North American Free Trade Agreement is one example of a trade agreement.

- International protest movements have also accompanied an increasingly global world, including Greenpeace, which works for environmental issues around the world.

Changing Social Roles and Relationships

The 20th century has seen significant improvements in human rights, including a reduction in gender-based or racial discrimination, as well as international condemnation of torture, unfair imprisonment and other practices. Discriminatory and unfair practices, like the Jim Crowe laws in the U.S. and the White Australia Policy, have come to an end.

- In 1948, the United Nations adopted the Universal Declaration of Human Rights.

Positive cultural identity movements developed, seeking not only to condemn oppression, but to celebrate identity. The French negritude movement, among French-speaking writers and artists of African origin is an example of cultural identity movements, as is the Black Panthers movement in the United States. While conditions have improved, on the whole, xenophobia remains, with discriminatory immigration practices, race riots, and the existence of neo-Nazi groups or racist groups like the Ku Klux Klan or KKK.

Religious movements diverged, in the 20th and 21st centuries in two very different directions. Secularism, or a lack of religiosity, became more common, particularly in Western Europe and some parts of the United States. In contrast, fundamentalism grew, both in parts of the United States and many parts of the Islamic world. These fundamentalist movements were more radical than mainstream religious movements and often involved in government affairs. New religions also developed in the 20th century, like the Hare Krishnas and various new age belief systems, but also cult-based movements.

Global Culture

With the innovations in media and communication technology, culture can now spread at a faster pace around much of the world. That culture includes movies, music, fashion and sports.

- The World Cup soccer tournament is followed around the world, with people gathering to watch it on television or the internet.

- Movies are translated and distributed from various countries to others.

- Music is shared and accessed from around the world. Global music styles may impact the work of different musicians.

Summary

- Key scientific and technological innovations include: automotive and air travel; radio, television, and the internet; antibiotics and surgical techniques; food production technology.
- The population increased, but war, disease and famine reduced the population at several points in time.
- Key global conflicts include World War I, World War II, and the Cold War. Students should also be aware of the Russian and Chinese Revolutions.
- Colonialism ended.
- Race and gender based discrimination was reduced and religious fundamentalism increased.

1. Compare the process of disease transmission and its impact during the Black Death to the impact of small pox on the Americas after the arrival of Europeans.

Low Scoring Essay

Both the Black Death and smallpox killed large numbers of people. The Black Death did so relatively quickly, while exposure to smallpox took significantly longer. There are a number of differences between the two diseases; however, both medically and historically.

The Black Death is a bacteria, commonly called bubonic plague. It caused a number of different symptoms, including large blisters. The Black Death was actually not typically easily caught from person-to-person. In most cases, the Black Death was transmitted through infected fleas, carried on rats by trading vessels, then spread over land, along the Silk Road. The Black Death had a relatively high fatality rate and killed 30 to 40 percent of the population of areas it reached, travelling through much of Asia, Africa, and Europe within just a few years. This is not the fatality rate of those that caught the disease, but rather the population overall.

Smallpox was a relatively common disease in Europe, Asia and Africa. While it was rather dangerous, many Europeans already had some immunity to the illness and it was not at all uncommon. Smallpox existed consistently, rather than appearing in a broad, fatal wave that spread across multiple countries. This was not true for Americans. The disease did not exist in the Americas and destroyed many Native American populations when they were exposed to it. The disease arrived in the Americas with European colonists, brought over by carriers on ships. This happened multiple times, prior to the introduction of vaccination for smallpox.

If people had not travelled, the risk of these illnesses would have been less. It is possible that they would have quickly died out, killing the portion of the population without natural immunity or the ability to survive. Today, smallpox has been obliterated thanks to vaccination campaigns and bubonic plague is rare and treatable.

Average Scoring Essay

Disease has frequently decimated human populations, altered lives and presented struggles, economically, medically and historically. Two of the most significant illnesses to strike humanity and cause historical impact are the Black Death and smallpox. The Black Death is a bacterial illness, caused by the transmission of the Yersinia Pestis bacteria. Smallpox is a viral illness, not unlike chicken pox, with several variations, some more or less dangerous.

The Black Death arrived in a fast and fatal rush in the middle of the 14th century, killing as much as 40 percent of the population from China to London to Baghdad and beyond. It moved quickly, taking only a few years to wreak havoc on the world. The path of the Black Death directly follows the trade paths of the late Middle Ages. It killed indiscriminately, taking both the rich and poor. With no understanding of how the disease was spread, there was no option for containment. The Yersinia Pestis bacteria is carried by fleas. Those fleas were carried by traders throughout the known world. They rode on rats in trading ships and on furs in the Silk Road, before finding and biting unwitting hosts.

Smallpox is a much more common illness. In some forms, it was quite mild, causing minor scarring, but no serious risk of death. In the most common form, it was fatal as much as 30 percent of the time, and almost certainly, more likely to be fatal for those in poor health. Some variations were fatal as much as 90 percent of the time. While worrisome, many in Europe had some natural immunities or had already survived a mild case of smallpox or a similar illness, to smallpox and survived it, perhaps with scars. This relatively common illness travelled to the Americas during the Columbian Exchange. The populations of the Americas had no natural immunity and almost certainly died at a much higher rate than Europeans, particularly after forced labor had physically weakened groups. In North America, smallpox blankets were intentionally provided to Native American groups with the hope of triggering infection.

Trade provided access to new foods, goods and labor. It also allowed bacteria and viruses to easily travel from place to place. For bubonic plague, this meant on rat hosts or furs, while smallpox travelled in human hosts or items they had handled, like smallpox blankets. The Silk Road, the Indian Ocean Trade Network and other trade routes spread the Black Death. Bubonic plague recurred later; however, it was not as prevalent, nor as widespread. Smallpox remained a scourge in Europe until the beginning of inoculation; however, its toll remained relatively low. This is not true in the Americas, where, eventually, smallpox and other European diseases wiped out native populations.

High Scoring Essay

Trade routes, like the Silk Road and, later, the Columbian Exchange, moved both goods and people long distances relatively efficiently. It was an even more efficient means to move diseases, like the Black Death and smallpox, across land, seas and oceans. While there are distinct differences in the pandemic of the Black Death and the epidemic of smallpox, both illnesses devastated populations and changed the demographics and landscape of entire regions.

In the 1340s, the Yersinia Pestis bacteria began to spread, moving outward from isolated communities in China. The Y.Pestis bacteria travels in fleas and was likely, at this time, carried on furs being exported out of the region. This bacteria can cause three different forms of plague. The most common is bubonic plague, causing large boils and killing approximately 60 percent of its victims. Other variations include pneumonic plague, which impacted the respiratory system, and septicemic plague, which affected the gut. Both have a near 100 percent mortality rate. Once Y.Pestis had reached more heavily inhabited areas, it spread quickly, with infected fleas finding rat hosts on merchant ships and caravans. The Black Death killed as much as 30 to 40 percent of the population of Europe in total, and similar numbers in other regions. For Europe, the Black Death and the dramatically lower population helped to bring an end to feudalism and welcome the new opportunities of the Renaissance. It is fair to assert that the Black Death ushered in a new and better age for many in Europe, rife with opportunity to gain land, pursue new employment and even become wealthier. Later waves of pandemic plague occurred, but without the severity of the Black Death.

Smallpox was a relatively common viral illness in Europe and other parts of Africa and Asia. The illness was well-known, but varied from quite mild to deadly, depending upon the variation. The most common strains had an overall mortality rate around 30 percent once contracted; however, in Europe and other parts of the "old world" many people likely had some natural immunity, either through genetic advantages or exposure to similar illnesses, like cowpox. Isolation measures were well understood quite early, limiting the danger of widespread contagion from smallpox in Europe. The same was not true when smallpox made its way from the "old world" to the Americas. Initially, it is most likely that smallpox arrived accidentally, as a sailor became ill on the ship or goods contaminated with fluid from smallpox reached American shores. With no natural immunity and depleted immune systems from harsh forced labor, smallpox and other European illnesses spread rapidly through Native American populations. While this early exposure was unintentional, later, smallpox was used as a biological weapon against native groups in North America. European settlers provided infected blankets to Native American tribes in the hopes of creating a smallpox epidemic. While the pandemic of the Black Death helped to create a newer, better Europe, smallpox and similar epidemics among Native Americans simply destroyed these populations, contributing substantially to the utter decimation of many groups. Faced with war, forced labor and a loss of land, the loss of population from an epidemic disease like smallpox was simply impossible.

While these two illnesses both have relatively high mortality rates and struck populations quite hard, the final impact on the individual populations was dramatically different. Europe came out of the Black Death to welcome a new era of experience, opportunity and learning in the early modern world. On the other side of the world, smallpox, influenza and measles destroyed entire cultures and civilizations, turning once great Native American cities into ghost towns and leaving only a few survivors behind in their wake.

Continuity and Change over Time

2. Analyze how the role of Christianity in society and government has changed from the time of Constantine to today.

Low Scoring Essay

Christianity has been the dominant religion in the western world since around 350 CE. It has changed over time, and has grown, as missionaries spread Christianity into Africa and the Americas.

Prior to the time of Constantine, Christianity was illegal and Christians were persecuted. Once Constantine accepted Christianity, churches were built and efforts were made to send out missionaries. The church grew and grew, but many of the leaders of the church were immoral. Because of this, the Reformation began, creating new churches based on the text of the Christian Bible, rather than Church tradition. Some countries, like much of Germany and Britain, converted to Protestantism. Others, like Italy and Spain, did not.

Christianity came to the Americas with settlers. In South America, that meant Spanish Catholics, while in North America, early settlers were Protestants. The founders of the Constitution acknowledged this Protestant tradition, but created a separation of church and state. That separation remains today, and is popular in other western democracies and Christian countries. This is better because it allows people to practice their religion without persecution.

Today, there are a lot of different Christian denominations. Some are very traditional, while others are quite modern. Traditional denominations maintain standard church services and may focus more attention on traditional values or even really old-fashioned ones. Modern services use newer music casual clothing and are often less formal than traditional services. The beliefs may vary, though, as belief and the type of service aren't always related to one another.

In this way, Christianity has adapted to the modern world.

Average Scoring Essay

Christianity was accepted by the Emperor Constantine and has grown since then to become a worldwide church. Jesus died in 33 CE, but it took around 300 more years for Christianity to become an accepted and well-organized religion and eventually, a force that ruled Europe. The Church was later divided, but the faith remained important. Today, Christianity, particularly Protestant Christianity, is growing.

In the first centuries of Christianity, Christians were persecuted by the Romans, limiting their political ability and authority. It is only after Constantine's conversion that the Church developed political power; however, during the Dark Ages, there was little political order or government. Christianity continued in the Byzantine Empire and North Africa. The Church helped to support the growing power of empire, as Charlemagne defeated various pagan groups and forced them to convert. Christianity spread rapidly from that time and was soon the dominant religion of Europe. The Church remained involved in government throughout the Middle Ages, even supporting the Crusades. The Church provided the only path to literacy, the only source of a university education and controlled rulers with threats of excommunication.

The Protestant Reformation divided the Church into a number of splintering smaller churches, including all sorts of Protestant denominations. This weakened the political power of the church and caused a number of conflicts. In practice, this provided a new incentive to read, new abilities for personal gain and new freedom for political rulers. Without the active presence of the Catholic Church, science was able to grow and thrive in many European countries.

The Enlightenment altered the impact of Christianity in Western society, creating a separation, for the first time, between religion and government. This spread and was embraced as part of an Enlightened government. Religion became a progressively more private and less public issue following the Enlightenment and became less prominent in society. While, throughout the 19th century and early 20th century, many were churchgoers, the church itself was less powerful. It had become a social tool rather than a political one. Many faiths took steps to modernize to meet the needs of their congregations.

Late in the 20th century, interest in devout and literal forms of religion, called fundamentalist Christianity, grew. Fundamentalist Christianity rejects many of the ideals of the Enlightenment and seeks a more active role for the church in government. These denominations reject modern social values, the role of the state and believe in a return to more traditional morality. While these are often associated with religion in the United States, evangelical movements are also growing in parts of Africa and South America.

.

High Scoring Essay

In the West, Christianity has shaped the world over time, just as the world has shaped the faith. From a small and persecuted religion, it grew into a force that controlled Europe, was divided by Reformation, and reshaped itself to meet the needs of a more modern world. Missionaries and trade spread the message of Christianity, and the faith adapted to the needs of local populations over time.

Christianity has its origins in the Jewish faith and finds its origin story, the Crucifixion, in the history of the Roman Empire; however, it is not a religion of the Roman Empire. Christianity developed in the hidden catacombs of the Empire, but was not accepted until the time of Constantine. For a short while, Christianity was flexible, without set texts or rituals and appealed, largely, to the lower classes. This changed as it became an accepted religion, embraced by the Roman state. Doctrine and acceptable belief were defined and the church split forming the Eastern Orthodox and Western Catholic churches. When Rome fell, Christianity remained.

In the early Byzantine Empire, the church was an intrinsic part of the ruling society, and as the Byzantine Empire spread, so too did the Orthodox Church. In the west, as learning and civilization remained in decline, the church remained, but was relatively small and weak. It gradually spread, through the efforts of monks, and by 800, it once again secured a clear relationship with government. The Church provided authority when it crowned Charlemagne Holy Roman Emperor. Later kings throughout Europe were crowned by their bishops, providing them with a means to authority from the Church. The Church was the sole source for education, authority, information, and more during this period, both in the East and West.

While the Church had been a key source of stability throughout the Middle Ages and Early Renaissance, in 1517, the Reformation began. The Church was, by this time, corrupt and battling a number of significant problems, including nepotism and the sale of indulgences. Martin Luther challenged many of these problems with the Church, originally intending to reform from within, rather than create a new church entirely; however, these challenges led to the creation of Protestantism, with its many denominations and varied beliefs. Protestantism weakened the position of the papacy, provided individuals with a new path to personal salvation, and altered the political climate of many countries and their relationships with one another. Now, a much wider range of religious options existed within a single faith, creating a much more multifaceted religion.

The influence of both Catholicism and Protestantism weakened as the Enlightenment progressed. The number of regular church goers decreased, and churches gradually changed their services to better accommodate their communities. In small communities, churches often remained a center of activity, filling a social function as well as a religious one. While the importance of religion decreased from the middle of the 18th century onward, by the late 20th century, the evangelical movement brought new life to Christianity. Evangelical Christianity favors a literal interpretation of the Bible, a return to a strong involvement of religion in government and has strong missionary tendencies. It is spreading rapidly, not entirely unlike the Church in a much earlier time.

Document-Based Questions

This collection of documents all relates to the French Revolution. Several are specific to Marie Antoinette who, in the popular press, bore the responsibility for many of the problems connected to the aristocracy and condition of the French people.

Analyze these documents and consider the causes of the French Revolution and how the royal family, and Marie Antoinette in particular, were involved in that Revolution.

Marie Antoinette. Letter to her mother, 1773.

On Tuesday I had a fête which I shall never forget all my life. We made our entrance into Paris. As for honors, we received all that we could possibly imagine; but they, though very well in their way, were not what touched me most. What was really affecting was the tenderness and earnestness of the poor people, who, in spite of the taxes with which they are overwhelmed, were transported with joy at seeing us. When we went to walk in the Tuileries, there was so vast a crowd that we were three-quarters of an hour without being able to move either forward or backward. The dauphin and I gave repeated orders to the Guards not to beat any one, which had a very good effect. Such excellent order was kept the whole day that, in spite of the enormous crowd which followed us everywhere, not a person was hurt. When we returned from our walk we went up to an open terrace and stayed there half an hour. I cannot describe to you, my dear mamma, the transports of joy and affection which every one exhibited towards us.

Madame Campan. Memoirs of the Private Life of Marie Antoinette, 1818.

In order to describe the queen's private service intelligibly, it must be recollected that service of every kind was honor, and had not any other denomination. To do the honors of the service, was to present the service to an officer of superior rank, who happened to arrive at the moment it was about to be performed: thus, supposing the queen asked for a glass of water, the servant of the chamber handed to the first woman a silver gilt waiter, upon which were placed a covered goblet and a small decanter; but should the lady of honor come in, the first woman was obliged to present the waiter to her, and if Madame or the Countess d'Artois came in at the moment, the waiter went again from the lady of honor into the hands of the princess, before it reached the queen.

Abbe Sieyes. What Is the Third Estate?

Public functions may be classified equally well, in the present state of affairs, under four recognized heads; the sword, the robe, the church and the administration. It would be superfluous to take them up one by one, for the purpose of showing that everywhere the Third Estate attends to nineteen-twentieths of them, with this distinction; that it is laden with all that which is really painful, with all the burdens which the privileged classes refuse to carry. Do we give the Third Estate credit for this? That this might come about, it would be necessary that the Third Estate should refuse to fill these places, or that it should be less ready to exercise their functions. The facts are well known. Meanwhile they have dared to impose a prohibition upon the order of the Third Estate. They have said to it: "Whatever may be your services, whatever may be your abilities, you shall go thus far; you may not pass beyond!" Certain rare exceptions, properly regarded, are but a mockery, and the terms which are indulged in on such occasions, one insult the more.

If this exclusion is a social crime against the Third Estate; if it is a veritable act of hostility, could it perhaps be said that it is useful to the public weal? Alas! who is ignorant of the effects of monopoly? If it discourages those whom it rejects, is it not well known that it tends to render less able those whom it favors? Is it not understood that every employment from which free competition is removed, becomes dear and less effective?

The Tennis Court Oath, June 1789

The National Assembly, considering that it has been called to establish the constitution of the realm, to bring about the regeneration of public order, and to maintain the true principles of monarchy; nothing may prevent it from continuing its deliberations in any place it is forced to establish itself; and, finally, the National Assembly exists wherever its members are gathered.

Decrees that all members of this assembly immediately take a solemn oath never to separate, and to reassemble wherever circumstances require, until the constitution of the realm is established and fixed upon solid foundations; and that said oath having been sworn, all members and each one individually confirm this unwavering resolution with his signature.

Declaration of the Rights of Man, 1789

Articles:

1. Men are born and remain free and equal in rights. Social distinctions may be founded only upon the general good.

2. The aim of all political association is the preservation of the natural and imprescriptible rights of man. These rights are liberty, property, security, and resistance to oppression.

3. The principle of all sovereignty resides essentially in the nation. No body nor individual may exercise any authority which does not proceed directly from the nation.

4. Liberty consists in the freedom to do everything which injures no one else; hence the exercise of the natural rights of each man has no limits except those which assure to the other members of the society the enjoyment of the same rights. These limits can only be determined by law.

5. Law can only prohibit such actions as are hurtful to society. Nothing may be prevented which is not forbidden by law, and no one may be forced to do anything not provided for by law.

6. Law is the expression of the general will. Every citizen has a right to participate personally, or through his representative, in its foundation. It must be the same for all, whether it protects or punishes. All citizens, being equal in the eyes of the law, are equally eligible to all dignities and to all public positions and occupations, according to their abilities, and without distinction except that of their virtues and talents.

7. No person shall be accused, arrested, or imprisoned except in the cases and according to the forms prescribed by law. Any one soliciting, transmitting, executing, or causing to be

executed, any arbitrary order, shall be punished. But any citizen summoned or arrested in virtue of the law shall submit without delay, as resistance constitutes an offense.

8. The law shall provide for such punishments only as are strictly and obviously necessary, and no one shall suffer punishment except it be legally inflicted in virtue of a law passed and promulgated before the commission of the offense.

9. As all persons are held innocent until they shall have been declared guilty, if arrest shall be deemed indispensable, all harshness not essential to the securing of the prisoner's person shall be severely repressed by law.

10. No one shall be disquieted on account of his opinions, including his religious views, provided their manifestation does not disturb the public order established by law.

11. The free communication of ideas and opinions is one of the most precious of the rights of man. Every citizen may, accordingly, speak, write, and print with freedom, but shall be responsible for such abuses of this freedom as shall be defined by law.

12. The security of the rights of man and of the citizen requires public military forces. These forces are, therefore, established for the good of all and not for the personal advantage of those to whom they shall be intrusted.

13. A common contribution is essential for the maintenance of the public forces and for the cost of administration. This should be equitably distributed among all the citizens in proportion to their means.

14. All the citizens have a right to decide, either personally or by their representatives, as to the necessity of the public contribution; to grant this freely; to know to what uses it is put; and to fix the proportion, the mode of assessment and of collection and the duration of the taxes.

15. Society has the right to require of every public agent an account of his administration.

16. A society in which the observance of the law is not assured, nor the separation of powers defined, has no constitution at all.

17. Since property is an inviolable and sacred right, no one shall be deprived thereof except where public necessity, legally determined, shall clearly demand it, and then only on condition that the owner shall have been previously and equitably indemnified.

Edmund Burke. The Death of Marie Antoinette

It is now sixteen or seventeen years since I saw the queen of France, then the dauphiness, at Versailles; and surely never lighted on this orb, which she hardly seemed to touch, a more delightful vision. I saw her just above the horizon, decorating and cheering the elevated sphere she had just begun to move in, glittering like the morning star full of life and splendor and joy. 0, what a revolution! and what a heart must I have, to contemplate without emotion that elevation and that fall! Little did I dream, when she added titles of veneration to those of enthusiastic, distant, respectful love, that she should ever be obliged to carry the sharp antidote against disgrace concealed in that bosom; little did I dream that I should have lived to see such disasters fallen upon her, in a nation of gallant men, in a nation of men of honor, and of cavaliers! I thought ten thousand swords must have leaped from their scabbards, to avenge even a look that threatened her with insult.

LaMartine. The Death of Marie Antoinette.

The Queen, after having written and prayed, slept soundly for some hours. On her waking, Bault's daughter dressed her and adjusted her hair with more neatness than on other days. Marie Antoinette wore a white gown, a white handkerchief covered her shoulders, a white cap her hair; a black ribbon bound this cap round her temples .... The cries, the looks, the laughter, the jests of the people overwhelmed her with humiliation; her colour, changing continually from purple to paleness, betrayed her agitation .... On reaching the scaffold she inadvertently trod on the executioner's foot. "Pardon me," she said, courteously. She knelt for an instant and uttered a half-audible prayer; then rising and glancing towards the towers of the Temple, "Adieu, once again, my children," she said; "I go to rejoin your father."—LAMARTINE.

Gabrielli. The Execution of Marie Antoinette

At 11am, she was led out of the prison, her hands bound and placed in the back of a cart that would take her to the scaffold on the Place de la Revolution. The way was slow, yet every account of her last journey tells us that she remained calm and composed. And as she reached the scaffold, she stepped down gently and walked easily up the steps. Then, she surrendered herself to her executioners and as preparations were made, every minute must have seemed like an hour.

At 12:15, the blade fell, and her severed head was held high to the joyous cries of the crowd.

The National Convention, 1792

M. Collot d□Herbois. You have just taken a wise resolution, but there is one which you cannot postpone until the morrow, or even until this evening, or indeed for a single instant, without being faithless to the wish of the nation, - that is the abolition of royalty. [Unanimous applause.]

M. Quinette. We are not the judges of royalty; that belongs to the people. Our business is to make a concrete government, and the people will then choose between the old form where there was royalty and that which we shall submit to them. . . .

M. Gregoire. Assuredly no one of us would ever propose to retain in France the fatal race of kings; we all know but too well that dynasties have never been anything else than rapacious tribes who lived on nothing, but human flesh. It is necessary completely to reassure the friends of liberty. We must destroy this talisman, whose magic power is still sufficient to stupefy many a man. I move accordingly that you sanction by a solemn law the abolition of royalty.

The entire Assembly rose by a spontaneous movement and passed the motion of Monsieur Gregoire by acclamation.

M. Bazire. I rise to a point of order. . . . It would be a frightful example for the people to see an Assembly commissioned with its dearest interests voting in a moment of enthusiasm. I move that the question be discussed.

M. Gregoire. Surely it is quite unnecessary to discuss what everybody agrees on. Kings are in the moral order what monsters are in the physical. Courts are the workshops of crimes, the lair of tyrants. The history of kings is the martyrology of nations. Since we are all convinced of the truth of this, why discuss it? I demand that my motion be put to vote, and that later it be supplied with a formal justification worthy of the solemnity of the decree.

M. Ducos. The form of your decree would be only the history of the crimes of Louis XVI, a history already but too well known to the French people. I demand that it be drawn up in the simplest terms. There is no need of explanation after the knowledge which has been spread abroad by the events of August 10.

Low-Scoring Essay

Marie Antoinette was the queen of France at the time of the French Revolution. She was quite selfish and continued to spend money even though the country was starving. She did not care about her people and can be blamed for the French Revolution. These documents illustrate the struggles of the French Revolution, from the ridiculous procedures in the French court to the final abolishment of the monarchy.

The first two passages, Marie Antoinette's letter to her mother and Camban's discussion of court protocols serve to show just how very disconnected the court was from the people. Even when, in a moment of kindness, Marie Antoinette insists that no one be hurt, it implies that people normally were. The amount of waste in the court had to have been unreal, given the number of people involved in dressing a single woman.

The Tennis Court Oath, Declaration of the Rights of Man and National Assembly piece all show how important the Revolution was. They set out smart guidelines to create a constitution and agreed that decisions about the monarchy should be made jointly.

The passages describing Marie Antoinette's execution suggest something very different about the Revolution. Marie Antoinette was imprisoned, tried without any proper legal defense, and sentenced to die. Her death is, after a life of parties, quiet only for her. She dies in front of a cheering crowd. Just as the queen died unfairly, so too will the Revolution die, after a Reign of Terror.

Average Scoring Essay

The French Revolution was a short-lived experiment, forcing a country from absolute monarchy to a republic in just a few short years. This was a violent process and one that took many victims, including Marie Antoinette, along with it. This isn't to say that the monarchy was a good situation, particularly for the lower classes, but that the Revolution was not, in the end, an effective solution.

The French court, as shown in Campan's passage, was an elaborate farce of ritual and routine. A young Austrian princess, Marie Antoinette, entered this court, hopeful and ready to start her new life. She did, as a young woman, care about her people, as expressed in the letter. She was not, as a girl, the woman known for her lavish spending. Even so, Marie Antoinette's spending was not the cause of the Revolution.

The king and Paris parlement summoned the Estates-General, or a meeting of all three estates, to deal with issues of government finance. When they did not comply with his wishes, he attempted to dismiss the Estates-General. The Third Estate refused to depart, taking the Tennis Court oath on the tennis court at the Palace of Versailles. They agreed to remain in session to create a constitution. The Estates became the National Assembly, creating the Declaration of the Rights of Man, based on the U.S. Declaration of Independence. Their work continued, with some conflict between those who wanted a constitutional monarchy and those committed to a republic, as can be seen in the records of the National Assembly.

With the final texts describing Marie Antoinette's death, it becomes clear who won in the Assembly. The former queen has fallen, been imprisoned and has been put to death. Her death is a public spectacle for a country already embroiled in revolution. With her, the monarchy meets its final end. Her children are motherless and her son will die from the conditions of his imprisonment in just a few short years. While her daughter will live out her life, it will be an unhappy one.

The worst days of the revolution are still to come, as many more will lose their lives to the guillotine. The deaths connected to the royal family are among the first blood lost during the revolution, but far from the last. Many more will die during the Reign of Terror.

High-Scoring Essay

The modern mythology of Marie Antoinette portrays her as a vain woman, completely removed from the problems of others, maliciously proclaiming "Let them eat cake!". Marie Antoinette never said those words, and as these documents illustrate, can be rightfully portrayed as a victim of her own circumstances, a scapegoat for the aristocracy at a time of revolution. These documents, as well as other evidence from the period, come together to form a picture of a troubled society, a spoiled, but not unkind, queen, and revolutionaries on a path to destruction.

The daughter of Empress Maria Theresa of Austria, as a young girl, Marie Antoinette was particularly noted for her fine character and gentle heart. Her tutors praised her many virtues, even if she was, on occasion, a bit flighty. The letter from the young Dauphine to her mother illustrates that. She worried about the well-being of the people and rejoiced in their joy. She is hopeful, kind, and, not long after her wedding, a much-welcomed addition to the French royal family. Raised in a casual and informal court, the rigor and rules of the French court must have been quite a shock to the young woman. As seen in the passage from Campan's book on Marie Antoinette, the court was highly ritualistic. A very young woman was suddenly thrust, not only into the limelight, but into a world of structure, rules and hierarchy. She had married a stranger and was, relatively early on, already failing at a key marital obligation, providing an heir.

Marie Antoinette made the French court her own, setting fashions from towering high hairstyles to simple muslin dresses suitable for picnics at her private country house. She spent lavishly, threw grand parties, and lived like a queen. As she enjoyed her status and wealth, the people of France were suffering. Eventually, the economic distress in France led to the beginning of Revolution, and the Estates Generale were called. Here, we find the words of the Abbe Sieyes regarding the Third Estate, the peasants and working class of France. He, essentially, states that the Third estate has borne the burdens of the wealthy and the aristocracy. Marie Antoinette personifies those burdens for many. Contemporary publications, including cheap pamphlets, portrayed her in the very worst light.

The French Revolution began with grand goals. The Tennis Court Oath marks the first sign of true power from the Third Estate, as they commit to remain together, working toward a constitution. Initially, the Estates-General worked with the king, but this marks a shift in that relationship. When the king attempted to disband the Estates-General, they refused. The power of the aristocracy was on the decline. The Declaration of the Rights of Man further emphasize the power of the people over royalty and the aristocracy. These rights have nothing to do with birth, so the rights that have traditionally been conferred by noble birth are irrelevant. They are also disconnected from the Church, suggesting the beginning of a newly secular society. The discussions from the National Assembly of 1792 illustrate the end of the monarchy. This is no longer a group committed to a constitutional monarchy, but rather moving rapidly toward republicanism. In this society, there was little room for a queen like Marie Antoinette, granted her position through birth rather than work. She was, fundamentally, a drain on the resources of France, rather than a benefit to it.

The passages by Edmund Burke, LaMartine and Gabrielli mark the end of the Bourbon dynasty, with one final death. Louis XVI had already been executed by guillotine and these passages all deal with Marie Antoinette's death. She was no longer a spoiled young queen. After years in prison, her health was failing, her husband dead and her children in danger. One had even been forced to make false accusations against her. Nonetheless, LaMartine and Gabrielli suggest that she went to the guillotine with grace and courage, revealing the character that her tutors and early letters had suggested. Finally, Burke's passage reflects upon not only her grace and beauty, but also her fall and, eventually, the fall of the French Revolution.

1. **In which country did the Industrial Revolution begin?**
    a. Russia
    b. Britain
    c. France
    d. The United States
    e. China

2. **The Red Army and the White Army are associated with what conflict?**
    a. The Civil War in the United States
    b. The Russian Revolution
    c. The Boer War
    d. World War II
    e. World War I

3. **What is a ziggurat?**
    a. A burial pyramid
    b. A Mesopotamian ruler
    c. A Mesopotamian stepped pyramid
    d. A temple
    e. A flat area used for Mesoamerican ball games

4. **In which region were alpacas and llamas domesticated?**
    a. Mesoamerica
    b. The Andes
    c. China
    d. Africa
    e. The Middle East

5. **When did horses reach the Americas?**
    a. With the first humans
    b. Around 5000 years ago
    c. Around 1000 years ago
    d. Around 500 years ago
    e. Around 8000 years ago

6. **When did Germany unite to form an Empire?**
    a. 1871
    b. 1914
    c. 1918
    d. 1891
    e. 1817

7. **Work on the Great Wall of China began in which dynasty?**
    a. Qin
    b. Tang
    c. Song
    d. Qing
    e. Ming

8. **The Boer War took place on which continent?**

a. Australia
b. Asia
c. South America
d. Europe
e. Africa

9. **Fascism is:**
   a. An authoritarian system of government.
   b. A form of racism.
   c. A government driven by racism or anti-Semitism.
   d. Hatred of Jewish people.
   e. A government motivated by religion.

10. **Which of the following is NOT associated with the Neolithic era?**
    a. Mudbrick architecture
    b. The development of pottery
    c. The domestication of animals
    d. The domestication of plants
    e. The use of iron weapons

11. **Who was Mao Zedong?**
    a. The last emperor of China
    b. The leader of the Chinese communist party
    c. The last democratically elected leader of China
    d. The leader of the Chinese Nationalists
    e. The first emperor of China

12. **Under the Roman Republic, who held power in the government?**
    a. The Senate
    b. The Emperor
    c. The people
    d. The Vestal Virgins
    e. The military

13. **Which ruler is commonly credited with Hellenism?**
    a. Genghis Khan
    b. Julius Caesar
    c. Nero
    d. Alexander the Great
    e. Herodotus

14. **Which of the following is most closely associated with ancient Greece?**
    a. The sonnet
    b. Drama
    c. Fresco painting
    d. Aqueducts
    e. Pyramids

15. **Choose the best explanation for the fall of Rome.**
    a. Rome fell to a superior military force.
    b. Rome fell due to the influence of the Christian church.

    c. Rome fell due to poor management, weak rulers, and an invading external force.

    d. Rome fell because it was morally depraved.

    e. Rome fell because of Caligula

16. **The Golden Horde was:**

    a. The name given to trade caravans on the Silk Road

    b. A famous inn on the Silk Road

    c. A type of glass, commonly traded

    d. The name given to the Mongol army

    e. The treasury of the Chinese emperor

17. **Which of the following was a prominent trading port in the Middle Ages and Renaissance in Europe?**

    a. Paris

    b. London

    c. Rome

    d. Naples

    e. Venice

18. **The building called Hagia Sophia has been both a Christian church and a Muslim mosque. It is located in what city?**

    a. Rome

    b. Ravenna

    c. Istanbul

    d. Athens

    e. Barcelona

19. **Choose the best description for the Russian strategy of empire-building?**

    a. Russia opted to colonize other regions, building a trans-oceanic empire.

    b. Russia spread its empire eastward into Siberia and west into Eastern Europe.

    c. Russia attempted to gain control of Japan.

    d. Russia remained isolated and avoided expansion.

    e. Russia lacked the resources to build an empire.

20. **The Treaty of Versailles:**

    a. Divided up Africa among the colonial powers.

    b. Allowed Germany to unite and form an empire.

    c. Ended World War I.

    d. Created the Triple Entente.

    e. Led to the declaration of war in World War II.

21. **Who first devised the League of Nations?**

    a. Adolf Hitler

    b. Woodrow Wilson

    c. Winston Churchill

    d. Kaiser Wilhelm I

    e. Franklin Delano Roosevelt

22. **Which of the following is an Enlightenment-era ruler?**

    a. Napoleon

b. King Louis XIV

c. Catherine the Great

d. Qin Shi Huang

e. Queen Elizabeth I

23. **The mandate of heaven is linked with the rule of what nation?**

    a. Britain

    b. France

    c. China

    d. Russia

    e. Japan

24. **Charlemagne was:**

    a. The last Roman Emperor

    b. The first Holy Roman Emperor

    c. King of France

    d. The first king of England

    e. A Spanish knight

25. **Choose the best explanation for the origin of the Byzantine Empire.**

    a. After the fall of Rome, the Eastern Roman Empire or Byzantine Empire became progressively more powerful.

    b. With Rome in danger, the Emperor moved the Roman Empire eastward.

    c. After the introduction of Christianity, Byzantium was founded as a Christian empire.

    d. Following the death of Muhammad, his followers created the Byzantine Empire.

    e. The Byzantine Empire began in Persia.

26. **What is a Janissary?**

    a. A Byzantine official

    b. An Ottoman soldier, born to a Christian family

    c. A diplomat from Persia

    d. A Venetian trader

    e. A merchant living in a community far from his home

27. **Select the best definition for diaspora.**

    a. The dispersion of Muslims from Mecca

    b. The dispersion of any group from their homeland, commonly in reference to Jews

    c. Trading communities of a particular ethnicity

    d. Roman communities set up on the borders of the Roman Empire

    e. Towns along the Silk Road

28. **What is social Darwinism?**

    a. The belief in evolution

    b. The belief that survival of the fittest applies not only to creatures, but also communities of people, particularly identified by race.

    c. A rejection of the theory of evolution

    d. The belief that evolution applies only to creatures and not social groups

    e. Belief in the Big Bang Theory

29. **Which of the following was first identified in the 18th century?**
    a. Vaccination
    b. Antibiotics
    c. Sterilization
    d. The shape of the earth
    e. Fertilizers

30. **Choose the factor that most significantly altered the food supply in Europe in the 16th and 17th centuries.**
    a. The potato blight
    b. The introduction of new forms of rice
    c. The introduction of the potato and other new world foods
    d. The use of new crop rotation
    e. The use of fertilizers

31. **What factor was most responsible for the decimation of native populations after the European conquest of the Americas?**
    a. Forced labor
    b. Disease
    c. Starvation
    d. War
    e. Forced migration

32. **Slaves were originally brought to the Americas to work:**
    a. Cotton plantations
    b. Sugar plantations
    c. Tobacco plantations
    d. In colonists' homes
    e. All of the above

33. **What goods were commonly exported from China along the Silk Road?**
    a. Silk, porcelain, jade
    b. Cotton and silk
    c. Silk and glass
    d. Silk, gunpowder and porcelain
    e. Silk

34. **The city of Jerusalem is holy to what religions?**
    a. Islam and Christianity
    b. Judaism and Christianity
    c. Christianity
    d. Islam and Judaism
    e. Islam, Judaism and Christianity

35. **Which of the following is the most ancient world religion?**
    a. Islam
    b. Hinduism
    c. Buddhism
    d. Christianity
    e. Judaism

36. **Choose the answer that best describes possible push factors for immigrants.**
    a. Access to jobs, land, economic improvement.
    b. Better climate, religious tolerance, stable government
    c. Poor job market, lack of opportunity, war, religious intolerance
    d. Communities of immigrants, family connections
    e. Expense of immigration, legal difficulties of immigration

37. **Traders visiting India brought what back to Europe?**
    a. Silk and porcelain
    b. Slaves and camels
    c. Horses and silk
    d. Cotton and spices
    e. Salt and cotton

38. **Maroon societies were:**
    a. Social groups for immigrants
    b. Escaped slave communities
    c. Abolitionist groups
    d. Enlightenment philosophers
    e. Groups to educate slaves

39. **The Holodomor was:**
    a. The mass killing of Russian Jews by the Einsatzgruppen
    b. Starvation in China at the time of the Great Leap Forward
    c. Starvation in the Ukraine under Stalin's rule
    d. The Russian Revolution
    e. Gulags in Siberia for Soviet political prisoners

40. **The Thirty Years' War:**
    a. Ended with the Berlin Conference
    b. Led to a political alliance between Sweden and Russia
    c. Decimated the German landscape
    d. Eliminated Protestantism in Germany
    e. Ended with the Peace of Augsburg

41. **Who was Marco Polo?**
    a. A Venetian explorer
    b. A Genoese trader
    c. A Spanish explorer
    d. A conquistador
    e. An Islamic explorer

42. **Which of the following is associated with the French Revolution?**
    a. The Declaration of Independence
    b. The Reign of Terror
    c. The Red Army
    d. Napoleon III
    e. The Battle of Verdun

43. **Which country or region invented the following items: gunpowder, printing, and paper money?**

a. The Abbasid Caliphate
b. Germany
c. Britain
d. India
e. China

44. **The Mauryan Emperor Asoka is associated with the spread of:**
    a. Hinduism
    b. Technology
    c. Buddhism
    d. Islam
    e. Literacy

45. **Women played a significant role in trade in what region?**
    a. Europe
    b. East Asia
    c. Southeast Asia
    d. Africa
    e. Mesoamerica

46. **The astrolabe is:**
    a. A type of compass
    b. A device used to determine distance over water.
    c. A device used to determine latitude on water.
    d. A type of calendar
    e. A mathematical tool

47. **Which African country or region remained predominantly Christian?**
    a. Zimbabwe
    b. Ethiopia
    c. Nigeria
    d. Egypt
    e. Algeria

48. **The Mughal Empire took its name from:**
    a. A region of India
    b. A Hindu deity
    c. Indian tradition
    d. A local river
    e. The Mongol Empire

49. **The Netherlands was best known as:**
    a. A political power
    b. A military power
    c. A trading power
    d. A site of religious conflict
    e. Fabric production

50. **Choose the best description for the agriculture of the Aztecs.**
    a. The Aztecs farmed on terraced land.
    b. The Aztecs grew wheat and rice.

c. The Aztecs grew corn and other crops on large reed mats in a lake.

d. The Aztecs imported food to cities over a long distance.

e. The Aztecs relied on large animals to plow their land.

51. **Select the best definition of mit'a.**

   a. Mit'a is a system of rule by the religious elite.

   b. Mit'a is a form of feudalism.

   c. Mit'a is a type of Aztec agriculture.

   d. Mit'a is a ball game played in Mesoamerica.

   e. Mit'a is a system of involuntary labor among the Inca, exploited by the Spanish.

52. **Which religious or philosophical beliefs are commonly associated with China?**

   a. Buddhism

   b. Confucianism

   c. Daoism

   d. Islam

   e. All of the above EXCEPT Islam

53. **Monasticism is associated with what religions?**

   a. Christianity and Judaism

   b. Judaism and Islam

   c. Islam and Christianity

   d. Buddhism and Christianity

   e. Hinduism and Buddhism

54. **The Abbasid Caliphate is closely associated with what city?**

   a. Constantinople

   b. Mecca

   c. Medina

   d. Baghdad

   e. Jerusalem

55. **Choose the best definition of Dar-al Islam.**

   a. The desire to spread Islam throughout the world

   b. The ideal Islamic education

   c. The overall spread or influence of Islam

   d. Islamic holy war

   e. The totality of Islamic belief

56. **Which best describes the difference between a serf and a slave?**

   a. Serfs had families, slaves did not.

   b. Serfs were connected to the land, not an owner and could only be sold as part of a land exchange.

   c. Serfs were freed after some number of years of service.

   d. Serfs were paid for their labor, slaves were not.

   e. Serfs were native-born, slaves were forced migrants.

57. **Who was Zheng He?**

   a. A Chinese Emperor

   b. A Chinese explorer

   c. A Chinese communist

d. A Chinese philosopher

e. A Chinese inventor

58. **The city of Machu Pichu is associated with what group?**

    a. The Maya

    b. The Aztecs

    c. The Olmec

    d. The Inca

    e. The Gupta

59. **The Bantu language and its descendants are associated with what region?**

    a. West Africa

    b. East Africa

    c. Southern Africa

    d. Southeast Asia

    e. East Asia

60. **Choose the best explanation of the Meiji Restoration.**

    a. The Meiji Restoration was an isolated, feudal government in Japan.

    b. The Meiji Restoration was an attempt at a nationalist government in China.

    c. The Meiji Restoration was an ancient Japanese government, influenced by Chinese tradition.

    d. The Meiji Restoration was the independent government of Korea.

    e. The Meiji Restoration was a modern, Westernized government in Japan, beginning in the middle of the 19th century.

61. **Which of the following describes a common trait in most of the earliest agricultural communities?**

    a. Stone and mudbrick architecture

    b. A walled city center

    c. Placement in a river valley

    d. The worship of nature deities

    e. The use of horses

62. **Which of the following did not have a state-sponsored or supported religion?**

    a. The Abbasid Caliphate

    b. The Byzantine Empire

    c. The Ottoman Empire

    d. The Song Dynasty

    e. The Maya people

63. **Why did Mesoamerican civilizations fail to develop the wheel?**

    a. They lacked the materials.

    b. They lacked the technology.

    c. They did not have large animals to pull plows or carriages.

    d. They did not have large scale agriculture.

    e. They did not have domesticated plants.

64. **North and South Korea were divided:**

    a. By the Chinese

    b. After World War II

c. After World War I
d. After the Korean War
e. By the Japanese

65. **Which of the following materials is most closely associated with the second phase of the Industrial Revolution.**
    a. Cotton
    b. Coal
    c. Steel
    d. Silk
    e. Wool

66. **Choose the best definition of the Green Revolution.**
    a. The Green Revolution was marked by a new interest in environmental protections.
    b. The Green Revolution was marked by technological improvements in agriculture.
    c. The Green Revolution was marked by reduced industrial emissions.
    d. The Green Revolution is a name for global warming.
    e. The Green Revolution describes a global movement to protect animals and plants.

67. **Which of the following statements describes both the French Revolution and the Russian Revolution?**
    a. Both originated among the wealthiest elites.
    b. Both valued the rights of the citizens.
    c. Both valued agricultural workers over the middle class.
    d. Both began in the bourgeoisie or wealthier members of the middle class.
    e. Both sought a totally egalitarian society, with publicly owned means of production.

68. **The first democracy was:**
    a. Rome
    b. Athens
    c. Sparta
    d. Constantinople
    e. St. Petersburg

69. **Confucianism is defined by:**
    a. Respect for authority, both familial and political
    b. A desire to reach Nirvana
    c. Respect for nature
    d. A belief that Muhammad is the prophet of Allah
    e. A personal desire for unity with the divine

70. **The Pax Mongolica protected:**
    a. Trade along the Silk Road
    b. Trade in the Indian Ocean
    c. The boundaries of the Mongolian Empire
    d. The boundaries of the Mughal Empire

e. The Mongolian Emperor

Free Response Questions

1. **Consider how colonialism altered the experience of native peoples over time, choosing one country for the subject of your essay. Depending upon the country you choose, the period of time may differ, but should begin with the introduction of colonialism and continue through the modern era.**
2. **How did trade develop on the Indian Ocean as compared to the Silk Road?**
3. **Historians have long argued over the origin of the Final Solution. Integrating what you know about Nazi Germany and the Holocaust, analyze whether or not the Final Solution was Hitler's original intention or a plan that developed due to the imminent loss of World War II.**

SS Himmler. Speech in Posnan, 1943.

I mean the evacuation of the Jews, the extermination of the Jewish race. It's one of those things it is easy to talk about, "the Jewish race is being exterminated", says one party member, "that's quite clear, it's in our program, elimination of the Jews, and we're doing it, exterminating them". And then they come, 80 million worthy Germans, and each one has his decent Jew. Of course the others are vermin, but this one is an A-1 Jew. Not one of those who talk this way has watched it, not one of them has gone through it. Most of you know what it means when 100 corpses are lying side by side, or 500, or 1,000. To have stuck it out and at the same time - apart from exceptions caused by human weakness - to have remained decent fellows, that is what has made us hard. This is a page of glory in our history which has never been written and is never to be written.

I ask of you that what I say in this circle you really only hear and never speak of. We come to the question: how is it with the women and the children? I have resolved even here on a completely clear solution. That is to say I do not consider myself justified in eradicating the men - so to speak killing or ordering them killed - and allowing the avengers in the shape of the children to grow up for our sons and grandsons. The difficult decision has to be taken, to cause this Volk [people] to disappear from the earth.

Goebbels, Diaries, 1942

Beginning with Lublin, the Jews in the General Government [Nazi occupied Poland] are now being evacuated eastward. The procedure is a pretty barbaric one and not to be described here more definitely. Not much will remain of the Jews. On the whole it can be said that about 60 percent of them will have to be liquidated whereas only 40 percent can be used for forced labor.

The Wannsee Conference, 1942

The Chief of the Security Police and the SD then gave a short report of the struggle which has been carried on thus far against this enemy, the essential points being the following:

a) the expulsion of the Jews from every sphere of life of the German people,

b) the expulsion of the Jews from the living space of the
   German people.

In carrying out these efforts, an increased and planned
acceleration of the emigration of the Jews from Reich territory
was started, as the only possible present solution.

Letter from chief of institution for feeble-minded in Stetten to Reich Minister of justice Dr.
Frank, September 6 1940.

Dear Reich Minister,

The measure being taken at present with mental patients of all kinds have caused a complete
lack of confidence in justice among large groups of people. Without the consent of relatives and
guardians, such patients are being transferred to different institutions. After a short time they
are notified that the person concerned has died of some disease...

If the state really wants to carry out the extermination of these or at least of some mental
patients, shouldn't a law be promulgated, which can be justified before the people - a law that
would give everyone the assurance of careful examination as to whether he is due to die or
entitled to live and which would also give the relatives a chance to be heard, in a similar way, as
provided by the law for the prevention of Hereditarily affected Progeny?

Testimony of SS private Boeck.
Extracted from "Der Auschwitz Prozess", by Hermann Langbein, Vol. I, quoted in "Auschwitz:
Technique and operation of the gas chambers - J.C Pressac, the Beate Klarsfeld Foundation, NY,
1989, p. 181:

Robert Jackson, Opening Remarks, Nuremberg Trial

What these men stand for we will patiently and temperately disclose. We will give you
undeniable proofs of incredible events. The catalogue of crimes will omit nothing that could be
conceived by a pathological pride, cruelty, and lust for power. These men created in Germany,
under the Fuehrerprinzip, a National Socialist despotism equalled only by the dynasties of the
ancient East. They took from the German people all those dignities and freedoms that we hold
natural and inalienable rights in every human being. The people were compensated by inflaming
and gratifying hatreds toward those who were marked as "scape-goats." Against their
opponents, including Jews, Catholics, and free labor the Nazis directed such a campaign of
arrogance, brutality, and annihilation as the world has not witnessed since the pre-Christian
ages. They excited the German ambition to be a "master race," which of course implies serfdom
for others. They led their people on a mad amble for domination. They diverted social energies
and resources to the creation of what they thought to be an invincible war machine. They
overran their neighbors. To sustain the"master race " in its war making, they enslaved millions
of human beings and brought them into Germany, where these hapless creatures. now wander
as "displaced persons". At length bestiality and bad faith reached such excess that they aroused

the sleeping strength of imperiled civilization. Its united efforts have ground the German war machine to fragments. But the struggle has left Europe a liberated yet prostrate land where a demoralized society struggles to survive. These are the fruits of the sinister forces that sit with these defendants in the prisoners' dock.

Government decrees against Jews, 1933-1936

When the Nazi Party gained control of the German State, the conspirators used the means of official decrees as a weapon against the Jews. In this way the force of the state was applied against them.

Jewish immigrants were denaturalized (1933 Reichsgesetzblatt, Part I, page 480, signed by Frick and Neurath).

Native Jews were precluded from citizenship (1935 Reichsgesetzblatt, Part I, page 1146, signed by Frick).

Jews were forbidden to live in marriage or to have extramarital relations with persons of German blood (1935 Reichsgesetzblatt, Part I, page 1146, signed by Frick and Hess).

Jews were denied the right to vote (1936 Reichsgesetzblatt, Part I, page 133, signed by Frick).

Jews were denied the right to hold public office or civil service positions (1933 Reichsgesetzblatt, Part I, page 277, signed by Frick) .

Resettlement of the Jews, 1943, prepared for SS-Himmler

The Auschwitz camp plays a special role in the resolution of the Jewish question. The most advanced methods permit the execution of the Fuhrer-order in the shortest possible time and without arousing much attention. The so-called "resettlement action" runs the following course: The Jews arrive in special trains (freight cars) toward evening and are driven on special tracks to areas of the camp specifically set aside for this purpose. There the Jews are unloaded and examined for their fitness to work by a team of doctors, in the presence of the camp commandant and several SS officers. At this point anyone who can somehow be incorporated into the work program is put in a special camp. The curably ill are sent straight to a medical camp and are restored to health through a special diet. The basic principle behind everything is: conserve all manpower for work. The previous type of "resettlement action" has been thoroughly rejected, since it is too costly to destroy precious work energy on a continual basis.

1. **Who were the citizens of the Roman Empire?**
   a. Anyone born in Rome
   b. Anyone who served in the Roman military
   c. All free men in the Roman Empire
   d. All men in the Roman Empire
   e. All free people in the Roman Empire

2. **Who was responsible for the conversion of the Saxon peoples to Christianity in the Middle Ages?**
   a. Constantine
   b. Augustine of Canterbury
   c. Benedict
   d. Charlemagne
   e. Boniface

3. **Vikings built a permanent settlement in:**
   a. Greenland
   b. Ireland
   c. Scotland
   d. Iceland
   e. North America

4. **A caravanserai was:**
   a. A camel saddle
   b. A guard for caravans
   c. An inn designed to meet the needs of caravans
   d. A type of carriage pulled by camels
   e. A trading post

5. **The first inoculation or vaccination prevented what illness?**
   a. Polio
   b. Bubonic plague
   c. Smallpox
   d. Measles
   e. Mumps

6. **Trench warfare was first used during:**
   a. The Thirty Years' War
   b. The American Revolutionary War
   c. The Napoleonic Wars
   d. World War I
   e. World War II

7. **The Crusades provided the west with one significant, positive and lasting consequence. It was:**
   a. Land in Jerusalem
   b. Improved hygiene
   c. Wealth
   d. Access to lost classical learning

e. A new understanding of medicine

8. **The elaborate examinations and qualifications associated with bureaucracy in imperial China are known as:**
    a. The Mandate of Heaven
    b. The Imperial System
    c. Confucianism
    d. Neo-Confucianism
    e. The Civil Service System

9. **Which emperor's actions led to the widespread conversion of the Roman Empire to Christianity?**
    a. Constantine
    b. Charlemagne
    c. Nero
    d. Justinian
    e. Augustus

10. **Where did monasticism continue to thrive during the period after the fall of Rome in Western Europe?**
    a. France
    b. Italy
    c. Greece
    d. Britain
    e. Germany

11. **Foot-binding was a custom associated with what country or region?**
    a. Africa
    b. The Middle East
    c. Southeast Asia
    d. India
    e. China

12. **The battles between Rome and what city are particularly famous?**
    a. Athens
    b. Sparta
    c. Persia
    d. Phoenicia
    e. Carthage

13. **Who was the first Roman Emperor?**
    a. Julius Caesar
    b. Caligula
    c. Nero
    d. Tiberius
    e. Augustus

14. **The Ottoman Empire was defeated by:**
    a. The Byzantines
    b. The Abbasid Caliphate
    c. The Crusades

d. World War I

e. The Germans

15. **Which of the following statements best explains the status of women in Tang Dynasty China?**

    a. Women were highly limited in their activities.

    b. Women had bound feet and could barely walk.

    c. Women had a relatively high status and more freedom than later Chinese women.

    d. Women were elevated in the courtly love tradition.

    e. Women were relegated to closed spaces and not seen in public at all.

16. **Choose the best definition for the Columbian Exchange.**

    a. The Columbian Exchange describes trading relations between Europe and the Americas.

    b. The Columbian Exchange describes the slave trade to the Americas.

    c. The Columbian Exchange describes the exchange of foods, people, diseases and goods between Europe and the Americas.

    d. The Columbian Exchange describes the trade in colonial properties.

    e. The Columbian Exchange describes the migrations to the Americas.

17. **A mestizo was:**

    a. A Spanish colonist in South America

    b. An individual with Spanish and Native American blood

    c. A slave

    d. An indentured servant

    e. A conquistador

18. **What was the First Five Year Plan?**

    a. A plan to create a communist state in Russia

    b. A plan to modernize the young Soviet Union

    c. A plan to industrialize Chinese agriculture

    d. A plan to stamp out western influences in communism

    e. A plan to expand the Russian Empire

19. **In what way did the Chinese and Russian Revolutions differ?**

    a. The Russian Revolution focused on industrialization, the Chinese on agriculture.

    b. The Chinese employed starvation as a control technique, the Soviets did not.

    c. The Soviets used prison camps, the Chinese did not.

    d. The Chinese tolerated cultural difference. The Soviets imprisoned those who refused to accept their ideology.

    e. The Russian Revolution was peaceful, the Chinese was not.

20. **The Umayyad Dynasty held control of a portion of Spain until:**

    a. The 12th century

    b. The 13th century

    c. The 15th century

    d. The 19th century

    e. The 20th century

21. **Which of the following best describes the Counter-Reformation?**
    a. The Counter-Reformation was a response to corruption in the Church that divided the Catholic Church.
    b. The Counter-Reformation was a response to the Protestant Reformation.
    c. The Counter-Reformation occurred in response to the discovery of the Americas.
    d. The Counter-Reformation occurred in response to growing secularism in society.
    e. The Counter-Reformation addressed the needs of the Catholic Church in the 20th century.

22. **The first university operated in:**
    a. Paris
    b. Bologna
    c. Baghdad
    d. Granada
    e. North Africa

23. **The capital of the Tang Dynasty was:**
    a. Beijing
    b. Shanghai
    c. Chang'an
    d. Nanjing
    e. Hangzhou

24. **Islam was founded around:**
    a. 600 BCE
    b. 600 CE
    c. 700 CE
    d. 800 CE
    e. 900 CE

25. **Tobacco and chocolate are:**
    a. Silk Road trade goods
    b. Indian Ocean trade goods
    c. Part of the Columbian Exchange
    d. Part of the Sub-Saharan trade network
    e. Rarely traded

26. **Coffee was a common trade good, frequently imported by:**
    a. Europeans
    b. Islamic regions
    c. India
    d. China
    e. Africa

27. **Human or blood sacrifice is commonly associated with:**
    a. Andean cultures
    b. African cultures
    c. Neolithic cultures

d. Ancient China

e. Mesoamerica

28. **The Louisiana Purchase, Mexican-American War and purchase of Alaska are examples of:**

    a. Imperialism

    b. Colonialism

    c. Aggression

    d. Isolationism

    e. Exceptionalism

29. **India was originally conquered by:**

    a. The British military

    b. The British navy

    c. The British East India Company

    d. The Dutch East India Company

    e. The Netherlands

30. **Which of the following best describes the consequences of the Opium Wars?**

    a. British occupation of China

    b. Chinese victory over Britain

    c. Unequal trade treaties, favoring China

    d. Unequal trade treaties, favoring Britain

    e. The British gained control of Korea

31. **The Raj refers to:**

    a. The government of Mughal India

    b. The British government of India

    c. The Indian Ocean trade network

    d. Queen Victoria

    e. The partition of India

32. **Mahatma Gandhi advocated:**

    a. The partition of India

    b. Indian dependence on Britain

    c. The creation of Pakistan

    d. Nonviolence

    e. Violent resistance

33. **Conscription is:**

    a. Voluntary military service

    b. Forced labor

    c. Coerced labor

    d. Forced migration

    e. Involuntary military service

34. **The invasion of what country marked the beginning of World War II?**

    a. Czechoslovakia

    b. The Soviet Union

    c. France

    d. Poland

e. Austria

35. **The Central Powers initially included:**
    a. Austria-Hungary and Italy
    b. Germany, Austria-Hungary and Italy
    c. Germany, Austria-Hungary and the Ottoman Empire
    d. Germany and Austria-Hungary
    e. Germany, Russia and Austria-Hungary

36. **The Warsaw Pact was:**
    a. A defense organization composed of the Soviet Union and Eastern Bloc
    b. A Polish anti-Nazi organization
    c. A Soviet alliance with Poland
    d. Soviet control over Eastern Europe
    e. The division of Eastern Europe after WWII

37. **Choose the best explanation for the blockade of Berlin.**
    a. The Americans were attempting to gain control of East Germany.
    b. The Soviets hoped to gain control of all of Berlin.
    c. The Soviets were trying to starve the Nazi administration.
    d. The Western Allies were hoping to capture Hitler.
    e. The Allies hoped to retake Berlin from the Soviets.

38. **What was the goal of the Gallipoli campaign in World War I?**
    a. The destruction of the Central Powers.
    b. The defeat of the Ottoman Empire.
    c. Capturing the city of Istanbul.
    d. Capturing Greece.
    e. Regaining control of North Africa.

39. **Which of the following countries claimed independence based on a slave revolt?**
    a. Cuba
    b. Brazil
    c. Haiti
    d. Mexico
    e. Jamaica

40. **Widespread civilian deaths in World War II, outside of the Holocaust, were largely the result of:**
    a. Machine guns
    b. Famine
    c. Air bombing
    d. Poison gas
    e. Trench warfare

41. **Ghettos, in the Holocaust, were:**
    a. Protected neighborhoods
    b. Traditionally Jewish neighborhoods
    c. Closed, overcrowded neighborhoods used to house Jews by the Nazis
    d. Concentration camps
    e. Death camps

42. **Select the best definition of the Caste system.**
    a. A defined, unchangeable social and religious hierarchy, determined by birth
    b. A changeable social hierarchy
    c. A religious hierarchy in Hinduism
    d. Hierarchy determined by skills and education
    e. A social hierarchy, determined by birth

43. **Siddharta Gautama was:**
    a. An Indian Emperor responsible for the spread of Buddhism
    b. A Buddhist monk
    c. The Buddha
    d. A Hindu author
    e. An Indian political figure supporting independence

44. The image portrayed here is a religious site. What religion produced this monument?
   a. Hinduism
   b. Buddhism
   c. Christianity
   d. Islam
   e. Jainism

45. **Choose the best definition of syncretism.**
   a. Syncretism is the blending of different artistic elements.
   b. Syncretism is the blending of different linguistic elements.
   c. Syncretism is the blending of different religious elements.
   d. Syncretism is the blending of different historical periods.
   e. Syncretism is a cultural blending that occurs through trade.

46. **What is a dhow?**
   a. A religious tax
   b. An Ottoman soldier
   c. A type of seafaring trade ship
   d. A Buddhist religious site
   e. A holy site in Islam

47. **Arabic numerals developed in what country?**
   a. Iraq
   b. India
   c. Saudi Arabia
   d. Egypt
   e. Tunisia

48. **Sufism is:**
   a. A Muslim tradition that follows descendants of Muhammad
   b. The government of modern-day Iran
   c. Islamic mysticism
   d. A Muslim tradition that follows the Qur'an
   e. Islamic law

49. **The word *dhimmi* refers to:**
   a. Muslims living in a Hindu state
   b. Muslims in a Christian state
   c. Christians and Jews in a Muslim state
   d. Jews living in a Christian state
   e. Foreign communities in trading cities

50. **A caravel was:**
   a. The transport of goods from place to place, commonly on the Silk Road
   b. The transport of slaves from place to place
   c. A type of trading ship used along the West African coast

d. A large ship designed by China

e. A ship used off the coast of South America by the Spanish

51. **If a state worked to increase exports as well as the supply of precious metals, it is pursuing:**

   a. Capitalism

   b. Mercantilism

   c. Communism

   d. Socialism

   e. Fascism

52. **Which form of Buddhism is most common among the general population?**

   a. Mahayana

   b. Zen

   c. Theravada

   d. Sunni

   e. Orthodox

53. **The Yuan Dynasty ruled in the 13th and 14th century and was created by:**

   a. Marco Polo

   b. Kublai Khan

   c. Genghis Khan

   d. Zheng He

   e. Hulegu Khan

54. **The African Songhai Empire:**

   a. Included Timbuktu

   b. Included Great Zimbabwe

   c. Included Gao

   d. Was located in East Africa

   e. Was located in South Africa

55. **John Locke was responsible for:**

   a. Government checks and balances

   b. The Declaration of the Rights of Man

   c. The social contract theory

   d. The French educational system

   e. The Glorious Revolution

56. **The Seneca Falls Conference was attended by which group?**

   a. Prohibitionists

   b. Suffragettes

   c. Abolitionists

   d. Agriculturalists

   e. Philosophers

57. **The Taiping Rebellion attempted to do what?**
    a. Promote Confucianism
    b. End the Qing Dynasty
    c. End the Song Dynasty
    d. Bring about a new democratic government
    e. Bring about a new communist government

58. **The Nuremburg Trials are best described as:**
    a. A war crimes trial after World War II
    b. A war crimes trial after World War I
    c. The rules and regulations governing the United Nations
    d. The creation of the League of Nations
    e. The laws that defined who was and was not Jewish

59. **Feudalism developed in:**
    a. Medieval China
    b. Medieval Europe
    c. Medieval Japan
    d. Medieval Korea
    e. Both Medieval Japan and Europe

60. **Which of the following is an example of a settler colony?**
    a. Australia
    b. Canada
    c. The United States
    d. New Zealand
    e. England

61. **The army of what country was responsible for the Rape of Nanjing in 1938?**
    a. China
    b. Korea
    c. Japan
    d. Vietnam
    e. The United States

62. **Collectivization is:**
    a. The transfer of land, farms and industry to public ownership
    b. The transfer of labor from free to serf
    c. The transfer of labor from serf to free
    d. Part of the capitalist economic system
    e. Part of the mercantilist system

63. **Who led the Russian Revolution?**
    a. Lenin
    b. Stalin
    c. Trotsky
    d. Alexander II
    e. Rasputin

64. **What is a theocracy?**
    a. A government led by the wealthy elites
    b. A government led by religious authorities
    c. A government led by a dictator
    d. A representative democracy
    e. A military dictatorship

65. **Fascism was NOT a system of government in which of the following:**
    a. Russia
    b. Japan
    c. Spain
    d. Italy
    e. Brazil

66. **The city of Tikal was built by:**
    a. The Inca
    b. The Maya
    c. The Aztec
    d. The Olmec
    e. The Chavin

67. **The Sand Road is sometimes used to refer to:**
    a. Land trade in Asia
    b. Land trade in Mesopotamia
    c. Land trade in Africa
    d. Trading ports in East Africa
    e. Trading ports in West Africa

68. **The Middle Passage describes:**
    a. The trade routes between Europe and the Americas
    b. The trade routes in the Indian Ocean
    c. The route slave ships followed from West Africa to the Americas
    d. Immigrant ships to North America
    e. Indentured servants moving to North America

69. **Choose the best definition of an indentured servant.**
    a. A slave with no rights
    b. An apprentice with many rights
    c. Someone who pays for his passage with a labor contract lasting several years
    d. Someone who becomes a slave through capture in war
    e. A paid servant

70. **Jesuit missionaries were most successful in:**
    a. Latin America
    b. Spain
    c. China
    d. India
    e. North Africa

Free Response Questions

1. How has communist China remained the same and changed over time, from the time of the Chinese Revolution to today.
2. Compare the impact of colonialism in India and Latin America.
3. The Mongol conquest led to great destruction, but also created a number of stable kingdoms that supported peace and learning. Using your own knowledge and the passages below, analyze the actions and goals of the Mongolian conquest.

Marco Polo. Of the origin of the kingdom of the Tartars--of the quarter from whence they came-- and of their former subjection to Un-khan, a prince of the north, called also Prester John.

The circumstances under which these Tartars first began to exercise dominion shall now be related. They dwelt in the northern countries of Jorza and Bargu, but without fixed habitations, that is, without towns or fortified places; where there were extensive plains, good pasture, large rivers, and plenty of water. They had no sovereign of their own, and were tributary to a powerful prince, who (as I have been informed) was named in their language, Un-khan, by some thought to have the same signification as Prester John in ours. To him these Tartars paid yearly the tenth part of the increase of their cattle. In time the tribe multiplied so exceedingly that Un-khan, that is to say, Prester John, becoming apprehensive of their strength, conceived the plan of separating them into different bodies, who should take up their abode in distinct tracts of country. With this view also, whenever the occasion presented itself, such as a rebellion in any of the provinces subject to him, he drafted three or four hundred of these people, to be employed on the service of quelling it, and thus their power was gradually diminished. He likewise despatched them on other expeditions, and sent among them some of his principal officers to see that his intentions were carried into effect. At length the Tartars, becoming sensible of the slavery to which he tried to reduce them, resolved to maintain a strict union amongst themselves, and seeing that he planned nothing short of their final ruin, they adopted the measure of leavingthe places they then inhabited, and proceeded north across a wide desert, until they felt assured that the distance afforded them security, when they refused any longer to pay to Un-khan the accustomed tribute.

The Journey of William of Rubruck to the eastern parts of the world, 1253–55, as narrated by himself, with two accounts of the earlier journey of John of Pian de Carpine.

Nowhere have they fixed dwelling-places, nor do they know where their
next will be... For in winter they go down to warmer regions in the south:
in summer they go up to cooler towards the north. The pasture lands without water they graze over in winter when there is snow there, for the snow serveth them as water. They set up the dwelling in which they sleep on a circular frame of interlaced sticks converging into a little round hoop on the top, from
which projects above a collar as a chimney, and this they cover over with white felt...And they make these houses so large that they are sometimes thirty feet in width. I myself once measured the width between the wheel-tracks of a cart twenty feet, and when the house was on the cart it projected beyond the wheels on either side five feet at least. I have myself

counted to one cart twenty-two oxen drawing one house, eleven abreast across the width of the cart, and the other eleven before them.

"I am the punishment of God...If you had not committed great sins, God would not have sent a punishment like me upon you." Genghis Khan

"The greatest happiness is to scatter your enemy, to drive him before you, to see his cities reduced to ashes, to see those who love him shrouded in tears, and to gather into your bosom his wives and daughters." Genghis Khan

"It is not sufficient that I succeed - all others must fail." Genghis Khan

Manuscript image of the attack on Baghdad in 1258.

The reply of Kuyak Khan to a Franciscan friar.

And when you say: "I am a Christian. I pray to God. I arraign and despise others," how do you know who is pleasing to God and to whom He allots His grace? How can you know it, that you speak such words?
Thanks to the power of the Eternal Heaven, all lands have been given to us from sunrise to sunset. How could anyone act other than in accordance with the commands of Heaven? Now

174

your own upright heart must tell you: "We [the Pope and monarchs of Europe] will become subject to you, and will place our powers at your disposal." You in person, at the head of the monarchs, all of you, without exception, must come to tender us service and pay us homage, then only will we

recognize your submission. But if you do not obey the commands of Heaven, and run counter to our orders, we shall know that you are our foe.

Marco Polo. This passage describes the court of Kublai Khan in the late 13th century.

It was in the month of November that Kubilai returned to Khanbalik. And there he stayed until February and March, the season of our Easter. Learning that this was one of our principal feasts, he sent for all the Christians and desired them to bring him the book containing the four Gospels. After treating the book to repeated applications of incense with great ceremony, he kissed it devoutly and desired all his barons and lords there present to do the same. This usage he regularly observes on the principle feasts of the Christians, such as Easter and Christmas. And he does likewise on the principle feasts of the Saracens, Jews, and idolaters. Being asked why he did so, he replied: 'There are four prophets who are worshiped and to whom all the world does reverences. The

Christians say that their God was Jesus Christ, the Saracens Mahomet, the Jews Moses, and the idolators Sakyamuni Burkhan [Buddha] who was the first to be represented as God in the form of an idol. And I do honour and reverence to all four, so that I may be sure of doing it to him who is greatest in heaven and truest; and to him I pray for aid. But on the Great Khan's own showing he regards as truest and best the faith of the Christians, because he declares that it commands nothing that is not full of all goodness and holiness.

1. **Minarets and calligraphy are associated with:**
   a. Hinduism
   b. Buddhism
   c. North Africa
   d. Islam
   e. Mesoamerica

2. **Kabuki Theater developed in:**
   a. Latin America
   b. China
   c. Korea
   d. Japan
   e. French Indochina

3. **Which of the following is not a similarity of the Haitian, U.S. and French Revolutions?**
   a. A declaration of human rights
   b. The desire for personal freedom
   c. The desire for increased rights for the working classes
   d. Violence
   e. Leadership by the well-educated upper middle class or elites

4. **Which of the following contributed to Nazi ideologies in the Holocaust?**
   a. Darwinism
   b. Christianity
   c. Judaism
   d. Social Darwinism
   e. Marxism

5. **Creoles were:**
   a. Individuals with Spanish and native blood
   b. Long term Spanish settlers
   c. New Spanish settlers
   d. Europeans born in Latin America
   e. Individuals with both European and African blood

6. **Vodun is an example of:**
   a. Shamanism
   b. Christianity
   c. Animism
   d. Daoism
   e. Syncretism

7. **In which of the following regions and periods did women have the greatest personal freedom?**
   a. Pre-World War I Britain
   b. The Soviet Union after the Russian Revolution
   c. China in 1800
   d. The United States in 1850
   e. Iran in 1981

8. **Choose the answer that is NOT an example of xenophobia.**
    a. White Australia Policies
    b. U.S. Reservations for Native Americans
    c. Religious tolerance in the Mongol Empire
    d. Immigration limits on Chinese immigrants in the United States
    e. Refusal to allow Jewish immigrants early in the Holocaust

9. **What is the Hajj?**
    a. Daily Islamic prayer
    b. Fasting during Ramadan
    c. Rules about contact between men and women
    d. Religious pilgrimage to Mecca
    e. Religious pilgrimage to Medina

10. **What was the Marshall Plan?**
    a. A plan to destroy Nazi Germany
    b. A plan to defeat Japan in World War II
    c. A plan to rebuild defeated countries after World War II
    d. A plan to help Britain rebuild after World War I
    e. A plan to defeat communism in Vietnam

11. **How was the Cuban Missile Crisis resolved?**
    a. The U.S. bombed Cuba
    b. The U.S. bombed the Soviet Union
    c. The Soviets removed the missiles
    d. The U.S. aimed missiles at Cuba
    e. The Cold War began

12. **The stupa is an architectural form associated with:**
    a. Hinduism
    b. Buddhism
    c. Islam
    d. Hare Krishna
    e. Christianity

13. **Labor unions developed:**
    a. Under communism
    b. Prior to the revolutions of 1848
    c. After the revolutions of 1848
    d. Early in the Industrial Revolution
    e. After World War I

14. **During the Partition of India, what independent states were created?**
    a. India and Pakistan
    b. A united India
    c. India, Afghanistan, Bangladesh
    d. India, Pakistan, Bangladesh, Afghanistan
    e. India, Pakistan and Bangladesh

15. **The Mughal Empire had a _____ majority and _____ ruling minority.**
    a. Buddhist, Hindu

b. Hindu, Muslim

c. Muslim, Hindu

d. Hindu, Mongol

e. Hindu, Buddhist

16. **In which of the following countries has religion played the smallest role?**

a. Russia

b. China

c. Britain

d. Germany

e. India

17. **Tanks were first used in what war?**

a. World War I

b. World War II

c. Vietnam

d. Korea

e. The Boer War

18. **While Germany was known for blitzkrieg warfare, Japan used what?**

a. The atomic bomb

b. Kamikaze pilots

c. Land forces

d. Trench warfare

e. Submarine warfare

19. **Population demographics are skewed and unusual in China because:**

a. Of starvation in the 1950s

b. Of the impact of the Rape of Nanjing in 1938

c. Of restrictive population policies in place since the 1970s

d. Of lack of access to contraception

e. Of lack of access to health care

20. **Between the 12th century and the middle of the 19th, Japan was ruled by:**

a. The Meiji Restoration

b. Samurai

c. A shogun

d. An emperor

e. A lama

21. **What facilitated the spread of Buddhism, Christianity and later, Islam?**

a. Missionaries

b. Emperors

c. Monks

d. Traders

e. Written texts

22. **By the beginning of World War II, Korea was:**

a. Under Chinese control

b. Under British control

c. Under French control

d. Independent

e. Under Japanese control

23. Why did the Silk Road eventually fall out of use?

    a. It was slow.

    b. It was dangerous.

    c. There were better, safer roads.

    d. Sea travel was faster and more practical.

    e. Trade stopped.

24. What event in East Asia do some scholars use to mark the beginning of World War II?

    a. The Rape of Nanjing

    b. The Japanese takeover of Korea

    c. The Japanese invasion of China

    d. The French takeover of Vietnam

    e. The Chinese Revolution

25. During the colonial period, Vietnam was under the control of:

    a. France

    b. Britain

    c. The United States

    d. China

    e. Japan

26. Which of the following is an example of large-scale architecture designed to illustrate the power of the ruler?

    a. The Ziggurat of Ur

    b. The Palace of Versailles

    c. The Stupa at Borobudur

    d. The Parthenon

    e. Hagia Sophia

27. Ibn Battuta, Marco Polo and Zheng He did NOT visit what location?

    a. China

    b. Baghdad

    c. India

    d. South America

    e. Africa

28. Lady Murasaki's *Tale of Genji* is:

    a. A defense of women's rights

    b. Epic poetry

    c. The first novel

    d. Written in Chinese

    e. A play

29. The epic of Malinke Sundiata is about:

    a. A mythological hero

    b. The founder of the empire of Mali

    c. The history of Mali

    d. A deity worshipped in Mali

e. The founding of the city of Ur

30. **The city of Timbuktu is commonly:**
    a. Associated with the founding of Islam
    b. Associated with the Ottoman Empire
    c. Associated with trade and education
    d. Associated with the slave trade
    e. Located in East Africa

31. **How did the Black Death or bubonic plague spread?**
    a. Sick people travelled for pilgrimages
    b. Rats carrying fleas travelled on trading ships
    c. Rats ran along the Silk Road
    d. Infested furs transmitted the disease around the world
    e. People transmitted it from person to person

32. **In what way did the slave trade differ substantially after 1500?**
    a. It decreased substantially
    b. It increased immensely
    c. Slaves were now from Africa, rather than Southeast Asia
    d. Slave traders were now local, rather than foreigners
    e. Slaves had more rights than before

33. **Slaves in ancient Greece were most commonly:**
    a. Prisoners of War
    b. Africans
    c. Greeks
    d. Turks
    e. Europeans

34. **Which of the following best describes the status of women in ancient Rome?**
    a. They had limited legal rights and powers
    b. They had full citizen rights
    c. They were isolated and unable to go in public
    d. They lived publicly, but had limited legal rights
    e. They were not allowed to be educated

35. **The Estates General refers to:**
    a. The French Revolution
    b. The French assembly
    c. Napoleon's empire
    d. The empire of Napoleon III
    e. The conference that met to write the constitution

36. **The technology of porcelain-making developed in:**
    a. India
    b. Mesopotamia
    c. China
    d. Japan
    e. Mesoamerica

37. **What innovation was necessary to support domestication of plants?**

a. The plow
b. The wheel
c. Animal harnesses
d. Carriages
e. Food storage, like pottery

38. Specialization of labor occurred:
   a. Prior to the introduction of agriculture
   b. Not long after the introduction of agriculture
   c. After the introduction of writing
   d. When humans developed religion
   e. After the industrial revolution

39. What is a quipu?
   a. Maya writing
   b. Inca record keeping
   c. Aztec writing
   d. Olmec record keeping
   e. Chavin writing

40. Napoleon's empire included which of the following regions?
   a. Italy
   b. Egypt
   c. Algeria
   d. Russia
   e. Morocco

41. Works of art from all over the world are in museums in the United States and Western Europe. Many of these were collected in the 19th century. What allowed these countries to acquire so much ancient art from varied regions?
   a. Imperialism
   b. The discovery of the Americas
   c. Mercantilism
   d. Capitalism
   e. Widespread migration

42. Large numbers of Chinese immigrants entered the United States in the middle of the 19th century. What is the primary reason for Chinese immigration in this period?
   a. They sought political freedom.
   b. They worked on the railroad construction projects.
   c. They were considered desirable immigrants.
   d. They had communities in West Coast cities.
   e. They were forced migrations.

43. What is subsistence agriculture?
   a. Agriculture on a large scale, with significant surplus
   b. Agriculture on a small scale, without surplus
   c. Ancient agriculture techniques
   d. The use of modern agricultural techniques
   e. Hunting and gathering

44. **Prior to the industrial revolution, what was the primary industry in India?**
    a. Silk production
    b. Cotton production
    c. Rice production
    d. Wheat production
    e. Subsistence farming

45. **The first factories produced:**
    a. Textiles
    b. Steel
    c. Coal
    d. Iron
    e. Steam engines

46. **What was the Lusitania?**
    a. A German submarine
    b. A British plane
    c. A British passenger ship
    d. A German trading vessel
    e. A German city

47. **Which of the following countries was the last to industrialize?**
    a. Britain
    b. Germany
    c. China
    d. Russia
    e. The United States

48. **Choose the best definition of feudalism.**
    a. In a feudal system, individuals owe loyalty and military service to a lord or noble, but farm their own land.
    b. Individuals owe loyalty and labor to the lord, farming both his land and a small plot rented from the lord.
    c. A feudal system is ruled by the Church.
    d. A feudal system is a type of monarchy, led by a king.
    e. A feudal system embraces slavery, with no personal freedom.

49. **The Nine Classics of Confucianism, calligraphy and poetry were essential for:**
    a. Chinese emperors
    b. Chinese concubines
    c. Chinese civil servants
    d. Chinese merchants
    e. Chinese nobility

50. **Apartheid was:**
    a. A type of slavery
    b. Strict racial segregation, associated with South Africa
    c. Trading practices in West Africa
    d. A form of colonial government
    e. Rebellion against colonial government

51. The Great Depression did NOT:
   a. Lead to significant inflation in Germany
   b. Impact countries around the world
   c. Impact Russia with the same intensity
   d. Lead to the New Deal in the United States
   e. Involve the stock market crash

52. Fascist governments can be characterized as:
   a. Theocracies
   b. Monarchies
   c. Oligarchies
   d. Authoritarian
   e. Military

53. The encomienda system was:
   a. A forced labor system employed in Latin America
   b. A traditional Inca labor system
   c. A form of feudalism
   d. A political system employed in Spain
   e. Religious persecution in Spain

54. Choose the best description of Spanish attitudes toward native peoples in South America:
   a. They viewed them as subhuman.
   b. They viewed them as a potential labor force.
   c. They wanted to destroy them.
   d. They avoided any form of interaction.
   e. They did not attempt to convert them to Christianity.

55. Which of the following is an example of syncretism?
   a. Latin American traditions involving saints and processions
   b. Protestant church services
   c. Decoration in Roman Catholic churches in Europe
   d. The reuse of Byzantine churches as mosques
   e. The immigration of Puritans from England

56. The Ganges River is closely associated with what religion?
   a. Buddhism
   b. Hinduism
   c. Christianity
   d. Judaism
   e. Islam

57. The Taj Mahal was built by:
   a. The builders of Mohenjo-Daro
   b. Asoka
   c. Malinke Sundiata
   d. A Mogul emperor
   e. Alexander the Great

58. The city of Rome fell to:

a. Julius Caesar
b. The Britons
c. The Goths
d. The Mongols
e. The Saxons

59. **How did the Byzantine Empire affect Russia?**
    a. The Russians adopted the Orthodox Church
    b. The Byzantine Empire protected Russian from the Ottomans
    c. The Byzantine Empire conquered Russia
    d. The Byzantine Empire fought Russia
    e. The Byzantine Empire did not affect Russia

60. **The Protestant Reformation began in:**
    a. Italy
    b. France
    c. Switzerland
    d. Germany
    e. Britain

61. **The Vietnam war is an example of:**
    a. The Marshall Plan
    b. Containment
    c. Communism
    d. Contamination
    e. The Domino Effect

62. **Following the discovery of the New World, Spain and Portugal were the primary explorers of the Atlantic. How was the Atlantic region divided between them?**
    a. Spain gained control of West Africa, Portugal the Americas.
    b. They each controlled what they could win.
    c. Portugal controlled West Africa, Spain the Americas.
    d. Portugal had trading rights and Spain colonization.
    e. Both had to have the permission of the Catholic Church to colonize.

63. **At what point did the Byzantine Empire reach its height?**
    a. Around 400 CE
    b. Around 550 CE
    c. Around 750 CE
    d. Around 1000 CE
    e. Around 1400 CE

64. **Where did the conquests of Alexander the Great stop?**
    a. Persia
    b. India
    c. China
    d. Egypt
    e. Mali

65. **The city of Mohenjo-Daro was located:**
    a. In the Ganges River Valley

    b.   In the Indus River Valley

    c.   In the Tigris River Valley

    d.   In the Euphrates River Valley

    e.   In the Yellow River Valley

66. After Britain, which nation was the next to embrace industrialization?

    a.   Germany

    b.   The United States

    c.   France

    d.   Russia

    e.   Japan

67. Which country supported the colonists during the American Revolution?

    a.   Britain

    b.   Canada

    c.   Mexico

    d.   Spain

    e.   France

68. Which of the following colonial states gained its freedom through violent rebellion?

    a.   Algeria

    b.   India

    c.   Pakistan

    d.   Bangladesh

    e.   Nigeria

69. Which of the following events in the last half-century was impacted by religious fundamentalism?

    a.   Indian independence

    b.   The Vietnam War

    c.   The attack on the World Trade Center on 9/11

    d.   The Korean War

    e.   The Cold War

70. The World Health Organization is:

    a.   Part of the League of Nations

    b.   Part of the United Nations

    c.   A global humanitarian organization

    d.   Run by the United States

    e.   Created immediately after World War II

Free Response Questions

1. How have interactions between the United States and other western powers and Japan changed over time and how have the cultural differences and values remained the same?

2. Compare the impact of the communist revolutions in Russia and China on the people of these countries.

3. **The Heian Period in Classical Japan is a time of remarkable learning, art and culture. The passages below illustrate more about this society, including the role of women. Analyze how these works relate to one another and to the culture of Heian Japan.**

The Lotus Sutra. 12th century Japan. Gold on indigo-dyed paper.

Sei Shonagan. The Beauty of the Seasons. 986-1000 CE.
The Beauty of the Seasons

In spring it is the dawn that is most beautiful. As the light creeps over the hills, their outlines are dyed a faint red and wisps of purplish cloud trail over them.

In summer the nights. Not only when the moon shines, but on dark nights too, as the fireflies flit to and fro, and even when it rains, how beautiful it is!

In autumn the evenings, when the glittering sun sinks close to the edge of the hills and the crows fly back to their nests in threes and fours and twos; more charming still is a file of wild geese, like specks in the distant sky. When the sun has set, one's heart is moved by the sound of the wind and the hum of the insects.

In winter the early mornings. It is beautiful indeed when snow has fallen during the night, but splendid too when the ground is white with frost; or even when there is no snow or frost, but it is simply very cold and the attendants hurry from room to room stirring up the fires and bringing charcoal, how well this fits the season's mood! But as noon approaches and the cold wears off, no one bothers to keep the braziers alight, and soon nothing remains but piles of white ashes.

Sei Shonagan. Women in Court.
I cannot bear men who believe that women serving in the Palace are bound to be frivolous and wicked. Yet I suppose their prejudice is understandable. After all, women at Court do not spend their time hiding modestly behind fans and screens, but walk about, looking openly at people they chance to meet. Yes, they see everyone face to face, not only ladies-in-waiting like themselves but even Their Imperial Majesties (whose august names I hardly dare mention), High Court Nobles, senior courtiers, and other gentlemen of high rank. In the presence of such exalted personages the women in the Palace are all equally brazen. Small wonder that the young men regard them as immodest! Yet are the gentlemen themselves any less so? They are not exactly bashful when it comes to looking at the great people in the Palace. No, everyone at Court is much the same in this respect.

Lady Murasaki. The Tale of Genji.
Tô no Chûjô nodded. "It may be difficult when someone you are especially fond of, someone beautiful and charming, has been guilty of an indiscretion, but magnanimity produces wonders. They may not always work, but generosity and reasonableness and patience do on the whole seem best."

Image from a handscroll of the Tale of Genji.

Fujiwara no Michinaga (966-1027) composed the following when one of his daughters became an imperial consort.

This world, I think,
Is indeed my world,

Like the full moon
I shine,
Uncovered by any cloud!

I preach with ever the same voice, always taking Enlightenment as my text. For this is the same for all; no partiality is in it, neither hatred nor affection. I am inexorable, bear no love or hatred towards anyone, and proclaim the Law to all creatures without distinction, to the one as well as the other.

I regenerate the whole world like a cloud shedding its water without distinction. I have the same feelings for the high-born as for the low, for the moral as for the immoral, for the depraved as for those who observe the rules of good conduct, for those of sectarian views and unsound tenets as for those whose views are sound and true. I preach the Law to the inferior in mental culture as well as to those of superior understanding. Untouched by weariness, I spread in season the rain of the Law.

Lotus Sutra

1. **The story of Romulus and Remus explains:**
    a.   The founding of Athens
    b.   The founding of Rome
    c.   The existence of the Roman Senate
    d.   The power of the Roman Emperor
    e.   The spread of the Roman Empire

2. **Which of the following did not support the transmission of diseases on a large scale?**
    a.   Bantu migrations
    b.   The Columbian Exchange
    c.   The Silk Road
    d.   The Indian Ocean Trade Network
    e.   Mediterranean Trade

3. **Read the following passage and choose the correct term for what is presented in this piece: "If anyone, no matter who, were given the opportunity of choosing from amongst all the nations in the world the set of beliefs which he thought best, he would inevitably—after careful considerations of their relative merits—choose that of his own country. Everyone without exception believes his own native customs, and the religion he was brought up in, to be the best."**
    — Herodotus, *The Histories*
    a.   Historiography
    b.   Cultural relativism
    c.   Historical fact
    d.   Personal narrative
    e.   Global history

4. **What does the phrase "white man's burden" refer to?**
    a.   The costs of trade
    b.   The expense of providing food and shelter
    c.   The burden of colonizing and westernizing "primitive" peoples
    d.   The costs of mining natural resources
    e.   The need to industrialize western nations

5. The image shown here is from the tomb of:
   a. Qin Shi Huang
   b. Wu Zetian
   c. Zheng Hi
   d. Cixi
   e. Mao Zedong

6. **Which European nation was particularly known for the strength of its navy?**
   a. Spain
   b. France
   c. Germany
   d. Britain
   e. The Netherlands

7. **Phoenician traders exported:**
   a. Cyprus wood
   b. Cedar wood
   c. Cotton
   d. Silk
   e. Porcelain

8.

This map illustrates:
   a. The Byzantine Empire
   b. The British Empire
   c. The Ottoman Empire
   d. The Napoleonic Empire
   e. The Roman Empire

9. **The most stable country in Latin America through the 20th century was:**
   a. Nicaragua
   b. Chile
   c. Brazil
   d. Mexico
   e. Peru

10. **NAFTA is an example of:**
   a. A defense alliance
   b. A trade agreement
   c. An unequal treaty
   d. A colonial agreement
   e. A global organization

11. **Who controlled trade on the Indian Ocean Trade Network?**
   a. The traders
   b. The Chinese
   c. The Indians
   d. The British

e. The pirates

12. **Piracy was common:**
   a. The Mediterranean
   b. The Indian Ocean
   c. The Atlantic
   d. The Pacific
   e. The Caribbean

13. **How does the Jamaica Letter, written by Simon Bolivar, differ from other declarations of natural rights?**
   a. It did not allow for natural rights
   b. It did not allow for personal freedoms
   c. It believed a period of dictatorship was necessary
   d. It supported a democratic government
   e. It attempted to create a free state

14. **What movement supported the revolutions of 1848?**
   a. Communism
   b. Marxism
   c. Socialism
   d. Capitalism
   e. Mercantilism

15. **Which of the following is an example of a theocracy?**
   a. Iran
   b. Iraq
   c. Saudi Arabia
   d. Italy
   e. France

16. **The United States backed which world leader in the 20th century?**
   a. The Shah of Iran
   b. Adolf Hitler
   c. Benito Mussolini
   d. Margaret Thatcher
   e. Tony Blair

17. **What is a "special economic zone"?**
   a. A region with lower taxes
   b. A region with higher taxes
   c. A colonial agreement allowing for trade
   d. An unequal trade treaty
   e. A region in China designed to encourage foreign investment

18. **Japan pursued a policy of _____ until the middle of the 19th century?**
   a. Mercantilism
   b. Isolationism
   c. Capitalism
   d. Imperialism
   e. Marxism

19. **The Crusades did NOT:**
   a. Result in lasting land gains
   b. Provide new learning to the west
   c. Offer an option for young men to reduce violence in Europe
   d. Provide religious indulgences
   e. Offer the opportunity to gain personal wealth

20. **The Heian Period marks:**
   a. The beginning of the Shogunate
   b. The end of the Shogunate
   c. The beginning of Classical Japan
   d. The beginning of the Meiji Restoration
   e. The end of Classical Japan

21. **Which of the following is not commonly correlated with industrialization?**
   a. Literacy
   b. High birth rate
   c. Steam power
   d. Internal combustion engines
   e. Lower birth rate

22. **Prior to the introduction of domesticated plants and animals ,humans:**
   a. Lived in large groups
   b. Built permanent settlements
   c. Had clear social hierarchy
   d. Were hunter-gatherers
   e. Were pastoralists

23. **Wu Zetian was unusual because:**
   a. He was a civil servant
   b. She was a poet
   c. She ruled as Empress, with full political power
   d. He explored much of the world
   e. She wrote the first novel

24. **The colony of Australia was originally established:**
   a. As a settlement colony
   b. As a penal colony
   c. As a French colony
   d. As a plantation economy
   e. As an American colony

25. **Educated native elites often returned to their home country and:**
   a. Assisted the colonial forces
   b. Served as bureaucrats
   c. Worked for independence
   d. Served in the military
   e. Immigrated to the colonial power

26. **Which of the following is NOT an example of colonial troops serving the colonial power?**

a. ANZAC
b. Canadian troops serving in World War I
c. Indian troops serving the British East Indies Company
d. Algerian troops resisting the French
e. Canadian troops serving in World War II

27. **William Smith paid for his passage by signing a labor contract to work under a blacksmith in the colonies. He will owe four years of labor, but expects to be a qualified smith at the end of his time. This is an example of:**
    a. Serfdom
    b. Chattel slavery
    c. Indentured servitude
    d. Forced migration
    e. Involuntary service

28. **Higher birth rates were more common in:**
    a. Agricultural societies
    b. Hunter-gatherer societies
    c. Industrialized societies
    d. Communist states
    e. Developed nations

29. **The Manhattan Project refers to:**
    a. The sale of Manhattan to the Dutch
    b. The development of the Atomic bomb
    c. The settlement of Manhattan
    d. The urbanization of Manhattan
    e. The creation of Wall Street

30. **Science and learning thrived under:**
    a. The Islamic caliphates
    b. Europe after the fall of Rome
    c. Europe under Charlemagne
    d. China during the Warring States period
    e. China during the Cultural Revolution

31. **Which of the following was responsible for many significant inventions, including paper money, gunpowder, and printing?**
    a. China
    b. The Umayyad Caliphate
    c. India
    d. Japan
    e. The Ottoman Empire

32. **What 15ᵗʰ century invention revolutionized Europe?**
    a. The steam engine
    b. The spinning jenny
    c. The printing press
    d. The damask loom
    e. The flying buttress

33. **Egyptian pyramids served what function:**
    a. Ritual spaces
    b. Burial spaces
    c. Palaces
    d. Symbols of power
    e. Living spaces

34. **Cuneiform and hieroglyphics are both:**
    a. Types of art
    b. Mathematical tools
    c. Epic poems
    d. Types of writing
    e. Types of buildings

35. **The _____ is to China as the _____ is to India.**
    a. Stupa, Pagoda
    b. Mosque, Stupa
    c. Pagoda, Stupa
    d. Mosque, Minaret
    e. Minaret, Stupa

36. **Which of the following cities provides insights into both Muslim and Christian history:**
    a. Athens
    b. Baghdad
    c. Timbuktu
    d. Istanbul
    e. Venice

37. **Which of the following is NOT a common trait of Islam and Judaism?**
    a. Use of a written religious text
    b. Reverence for prophets of God
    c. A requirement of a religious pilgrimage to Mecca
    d. Holy sites in Jerusalem
    e. A traditionally patriarchal culture

38. **The Phoenicians were responsible for what achievement:**
    a. Cuneiform
    b. Hieroglyphs
    c. Pictograms
    d. Phonetic alphabet
    e. The dhow

39. **Choose the best description of early trade networks in the Americas:**
    a. They were well-organized and large
    b. They were minimal and local
    c. They traded large scale goods
    d. There was no trade in the Americas
    e. They traded with European explorers

40. **One distinctive architectural form has developed in various locations around the world, independently. It is:**

a. The stupa
b. The minaret
c. The gothic cathedral
d. The skyscraper
e. The stepped pyramid

41. The Spanish Inquisition was:

a. An attempt to weed out heresy in the Catholic Church
b. An attempt to reduce abuses within the Church
c. A response to the Protestant Reformation
d. A response to the discovery of the Americas
e. Devised by King Ferdinand and Queen Isabella

42. The Taiping Rebellion hoped to overthrow the Qing Dynasty and:

a. Establish Daoism
b. Establish Buddhism
c. Establish Confucianism
d. Establish Christianity
e. Establish Islam

43. Areas of Africa that are were not successfully converted to either Islam or Christianity practice:

a. Vodun
b. Buddhism
c. Hinduism
d. Shamanism
e. Daoism

44. How did the Phoenician trade network end?

a. The Phoenicians were defeated by Rome
b. The Phoenicians died from disease
c. The Phoenicians settled a new land
d. The Phoenicians stopped trading
e. The Phoenicians were defeated by Athens

45. Rome idolized the culture of:

a. Britain
b. Phoenicia
c. The Iliad
d. Egypt
e. Greece

46. What is asceticism?

a. Self-denial
b. Self-indulgence
c. Self-harm
d. Isolation
e. A religious tradition

47. Plato and Aristotle are examples of:

a. Greek playwrights

b. Greek epic poets

c. Greek ship builders

d. Greek philosophers

e. Greek politicians

48. **Contact between Russia and Europe began:**

a. After the Russian Revolution

b. During World War I

c. With the reign of Peter the Great

d. With the reign of Catherine the Great

e. With the reign of Alexander II

49. **Which of the following cities had the closest ties to the Byzantine Empire?**

a. Venice

b. Paris

c. London

d. Rome

e. Baghdad

50. **Sugar plantations were most commonly located:**

a. In India

b. In South America

c. In the Caribbean

d. In North America

e. In Central America

51. **Christian monasticism has its origins:**

a. In Britain

b. In Italy

c. In Greece

d. In Egypt

e. In Jerusalem

52. **The Yin-Yang symbol is part of what tradition:**

a. Confucianism

b. Buddhism

c. Daoism

d. Hinduism

e. Islam

53. **The encomienda system is most similar to which of the following:**

a. Mercantilism

b. Marxism

c. Chattel slavery

d. Manorialism

e. Authoritarianism

54. **What criteria was used to divide India when it was partitioned?**

a. Language

b. Ethnicity

c. Natural boundaries

d. Religion

e. Colonial boundaries

55. **What is eremitism?**

a. Self-denial

b. Self-isolation

c. Self-flagellation

d. Self-immolation

e. Self-discipline

56. **How did political stability or instability impact trade along the Silk Road?**

a. Stable imperial rule allowed for easier trade and travel.

b. Political instability made trading more profitable.

c. Political stability led traders to use sea routes.

d. Political conditions did not impact the trade routes.

e. Political instability led to a lack of international trade

57. **Identify the primary source from the list below:**

a. A novel about the Byzantine Empire

b. A diary of a lady of the court during the French Revolution

c. A historical textbook about the Russian Revolution

d. A movie made about the Chinese Revolution

e. A documentary about the French Revolution

58. **Choose the answer that presents events in the correct chronology:**

a. The French Revolution, the American Revolution, the Industrial Revolution, World War I

b. The American Revolution, the French Revolution, Napoleon, World War I

c. The French Revolution, Napoleon, the American Revolution, World War I

d. Napoleon, the intervention of the steam engine, World War I, the invention of the automobile

e. The Rape of Nanjing, World War I, the Great Depression, World War II

59. **Choose the best definition for nepotism:**

a. Awarding jobs based on merit

b. Awarding jobs based on test scores

c. Awarding jobs based on personal connections

d. Awarding jobs based on bribery

e. Awarding jobs based on a combination of merit and scores

60. **In the Chinese family, traditionally, who holds authority?**

a. The mother

b. The grandmother

c. The father

d. The children

e. The manorial lord

61. **Where was the conference held that divided the city of Berlin and other lands near the end of World War II?**

a. Berlin

b. Dresden

c. Paris
d. Yalta
e. Athens

62. **The Glorious Revolution occurred in:**
    a. France
    b. America
    c. Haiti
    d. Britain
    e. Jamaica

63. **The Boxer Rebellion was opposed to:**
    a. Foreign influences
    b. Chinese imperialism
    c. Japanese imperialism
    d. Korean imperialism
    e. Buddhism

64. **What Roman general conquered modern-day France and portions of Britain?**
    a. Trajan
    b. Julius Caesar
    c. Nero
    d. Caligula
    e. Augustus

65. **The Ottoman Empire did NOT recognize which of the following religions?**
    a. Orthodox Christianity
    b. Judaism
    c. Sunni Islam
    d. Shi'a Islam
    e. Armenian Christians

66. **Between 1915 and 1922, Turkey forced Armenian Christians from their homes, forced them to march into the desert, killed many, and forcibly kidnapped and converted Armenian children. This is an example of:**
    a. Religious persecution
    b. Holodomor
    c. Holocaust
    d. Genocide
    e. Fascism

67. **What international incident set off World War I?**
    a. The invasion of Poland
    b. The attack on Serbia
    c. The assassination of Archduke Ferdinand
    d. The attack on Belgium
    e. The attack on Russia

68. **The city of Persepolis was:**
    a. In Greece
    b. In Turkey

    c.   In Phoenicia

    d.   In Syria

    e.   In Persia

69. One South American country has been ruled by a monarch. It is:

    a.   Chile

    b.   Peru

    c.   Brazil

    d.   Colombia

    e.   Uruguay

70. Which African nation retained its independence?

    a.   Zaire

    b.   Nigeria

    c.   Ethiopia

    d.   South Africa

    e.   Mali

Free Response Questions

1. **How has Islam changed or remained the same, in terms of action, expectation, beliefs, and values, since its inception in 622 CE?**

2. **Compare the Abbasid Caliphate to Western European society in the Middle Ages.**

3. **The following passages describe the actions of Europeans with regard to Africans, including the experiences of a British traveler, a discussion of slave ships, and explanations of white burden. Analyze these passages and consider how these texts reflect changing views of Africa over time.**

Richard Eden's Decades of the New World, 1555

Touching the manners and nature of the people, this may seem strange, that their princes and noblemen used to pounce and raise their skins with pretty knots in diverse forms, as it were branched damask, thinking that to be a decent ornament. And albeit they go in manner all naked, yet are many of them, and especially their women, in manner laden with collars, bracelets, hoops and chains, either of gold, copper, or ivory. I myself have one of their bracelets of ivory, weighing two pound and six ounces of troy weight, which make eight and thirty ounces. This one of their women did wear upon her arm. It is made of one whole piece of the biggest part of the tooth, turned and somewhat carved, with a hole in the midst, wherein they put their hands to wear it on their arm. Some have on every arm one, and as many on their legs, wherewith some of them are so galled that, although they are in manner made lame thereby, yet will they by no means leave them off. Some wear also on their legs great shackles of bright copper, which they think to be no less comely. They wear also collars, bracelets, garlands and girdles, of certain blue stones like beads. Likewise, some of their women wear on their bare arms certain foresleeves made of the plates of beaten gold. On their fingers also they wear rings, made of golden wires, with a knot or wreath, like unto that which children make in a ring of a rush. Among other things of gold, that our men bought of them for exchange of their wares, were certain dog-chains and collars.

They are very wary people in their bargaining, and will not lose one spark of gold of any value. They use weights and measures, and are very circumspect in occupying the same. They that shall have to do with them, must use them gently; for they will not traffic or bring in any wares, if they be evil used.

John Barbot, 1732, Slave Trade Documents

John Barbot traveled at least twice to the West Coast of Africa (in 1678 and 1682) for the French Royal African Company.

Those sold by the Blacks are for the most part prisoners of war, taken either in fight, or pursuit, or in the incursions they make into their enemies territories; others stolen away by their own countrymen; and some there are, who will sell their own children, kindred, or neighbours. This has been often seen, and to compass it, they desire the person they intend to sell, to help them in carrying something to the factory by way of trade, and when there, the person so deluded, not understanding the language, is old and deliver'd up as a slave, notwithstanding all his resistance, and exclaiming against the treachery....

The kings are so absolute, that upon any slight pretense of offences committed by their subjects, they order them to be sold for slaves, without regard to rank, or possession....

Alexander Falconbridge, a surgeon aboard slave ships and later the governor of a British colony for freed slaves in Sierra Leone, gives this account of the Middle Passage.

From the time of the arrival of the ships to their departure, which is usually about three months, scarce a day passes without some Negroes being purchased and carried on board; sometimes in small and sometimes in large numbers. The whole number taken on board depends on circumstances. In a voyage I once made, our stock of merchandise was exhausted in the purchase of about 380 Negroes, which was expected to have procured 500...

The men Negroes, on being brought aboard the ship, are immediately fastened together, two and two, by handcuffs on their wrists and by irons riveted on their legs. They are then sent down between the decks and placed in an apartment partitioned off for that purpose. The women also are placed in a separate apartment between the decks, but without being ironed. An adjoining room on the same deck is appointed for the boys. Thus they are all placed in different apartments.

But at the same time, however, they are frequently stowed so close, as to admit of no other position than lying on their sides. Nor with the height between decks, unless directly under the grating, permit the indulgence of an erect posture; especially where there are platforms, which is generally the case. These platforms are a kind of shelf, about eight or nine feet in breadth, extending from the side of the ship toward the centre. They are placed nearly midway between the decks, at the distance of two or three feet from each deck. Upon these the Negroes are stowed in the same manner as they are on the deck underneath.

In each of the apartments are placed three or four large buckets, of a conical form, nearly two feet in diameter at the bottom and only one foot at the top and in depth of about twenty-eight inches, to which, when necessary, the Negroes have recourse. It often happens that those who are placed at a distance from the buckets, in endeavoring to get to them, tumble over their companions, in consequence of their being shackled. These accidents, although unavoidable, are productive of continual quarrels in which some of them are always bruised. In this distressed situation, unable to proceed and prevented from getting to the tubs, they desist from the attempt; and as the necessities of nature are not to be resisted, ease themselves as they lie. This becomes a fresh source of boils and disturbances and tends to render the condition of the poor captive wretches still more uncomfortable. The nuisance arising from these circumstances is not infrequently increased by the tubs being too small for the purpose intended and their being emptied but once every day. The rule for doing so, however, varies in different ships according to the attention paid to the health and convenience of the slaves by the captain. . . .

Upon the Negroes refusing to take sustenance, I have seen coals of fire, glowing hot, put on a shovel and placed so near their lips as to scorch and burn them. And this has been accompanied with threats of forcing them to swallow the coals if they any longer persisted in refusing to eat. These means have generally had the desired effect. I have also been credibly informed that a certain captain in the slave-trade, poured melted lead on such of his Negroes as obstinately refused their food. . . .

203

This poem is symbolic of the imperial adventure, expressing the European—here, British—belief that non-European countries needed European "guidance" in the form of paternalism, one facet of colonialism.

Take up the White Man's burden--

Send forth the best ye breed--

Go bind your sons to exile

To serve your captives' need;

To wait in heavy harness,

On fluttered folk and wild--

Your new-caught, sullen peoples,

Half-devil and half-child.

Take up the White Man's Burden--

In patience to abide,

To veil the threat of terror

And check the show of pride;

By open speech and simple,

An hundred times made plain.

To seek another's profit,

And work another's gain.

Take up the White Man's burden--

The following response to Kipling's poem The White Man's Burden, *was written in 1903 by the British journalist Edward Morel based on his experiences in the Belgian Congo; it highlighted the abuse suffered in Africa due to European colonialism.*

It is [the Africans] who carry the 'Black man's burden'. They have not withered away before the white man's occupation. Indeed ... Africa has ultimately absorbed within itself every Caucasian and, for that matter, every Semitic invader, too. In hewing out for himself a fixed abode in

Africa, the white man has massacred the African in heaps. The African has survived, and it is well for the white settlers that he has....

What the partial occupation of his soil by the white man has failed to do; what the mapping out of European political 'spheres of influence' has failed to do; what the Maxim and the rifle, the slave gang, labour in the bowels of the earth and the lash, have failed to do; what imported measles, smallpox and syphilis have failed to do; whatever the overseas slave trade failed to do, the power of modern capitalistic exploitation, assisted by modern engines of destruction, may yet succeed in accomplishing.

Answer Key 1

1. B
2. B
3. C
4. B
5. D
6. A
7. A
8. E
9. A
10. E
11. B
12. A
13. D
14. B
15. C
16. D
17. E
18. C
19. B
20. C
21. B
22. C
23. C
24. B
25. A
26. B
27. B
28. B
29. A
30. C
31. B
32. B
33. A
34. E
35. B
36. C
37. D
38. B
39. C
40. C
41. A
42. B
43. E

44. C
45. C
46. C
47. B
48. E
49. C
50. C
51. E
52. E
53. D
54. D
55. C
56. B
57. B
58. D
59. C
60. E
61. C
62. D
63. C
64. B
65. C
66. B
67. D
68. B
69. A
70. A

1. **Consider how colonialism altered the experience of native peoples over time, choosing one country for the subject of your essay. Depending upon the country you choose, the period of time may differ, but should begin with the introduction of colonialism and continue through the modern era.**

In 1490, the native peoples of Mesoamerica, including the Aztec, were strong, technologically developed civilizations. They built monumental architecture, fought, lived, farmed, and thrived in the lush climate, from the city of Tenochtitlan to the smaller towns. Their cultures, both that of the Aztecs and those of their enemies, were old, strong and well-developed, but they fell and fell quickly to the guns, horses and diseases brought by Spanish conquistadors and their native allies in Mesoamerica.

The invasion in 1519 led to the capture of the leader of the Aztecs and eventually their defeat. While there were a number of battles, the Spanish conquistadors had another distinct advantage. Smallpox had reached the Aztec communities around the same time, killing as much as 50 percent of the population. With the defeat of the Aztecs, the most powerful warriors in the region, the Spanish conquistadors had secured their control of modern-day Mexico. After the fall of the Aztecs, the Spanish renamed the region New Spain.

While many of the Aztec nobility were killed by conquistadors, those that remained held a relatively high social status, continuing their traditional role to a lesser extent. They were referred to by Spanish noble titles, including don and dona. Some learned Spanish, and many converted to Christianity, after regular interactions with Jesuit missionaries. While Aztec nobles retained some status, the Spanish implemented the encomienda system, a forced labor system resembling feudalism. This was based in both South American and European traditions, but adapted for the colonial world. In Europe, feudalism had disappeared, altering the face of Europe.

Conditions for forced laborers were quite poor, both those working in agriculture and those in the mines. Spanish men who settled in New Spain frequently married native women or took native concubines, creating the new class known as mestizos. While the mestizos were, by blood, both Spanish and Aztec, the culture and traditions of the Aztecs were largely rejected and were, in many cases, illegal. While the mestizos lacked the social status of the creoles or new settlers, they could attain a high social status and role.

For the Spanish, the Aztecs were less than, but were not subhuman. Mendicant friars, including the Dominicans and Franciscans, believed that they could be converted and could benefit the Catholic Church. The introduction of smallpox was unintentional, but certainly advantageous, helping the Spanish to secure their victory. While forced laborers were not well-treated and were often abused, they were not slaves and there was no intentional attempt to destroy the Aztec population; however, the actions of the Spanish destroyed the Aztec way of life and culture.

2. How did trade develop on the Indian Ocean as compared to the Silk Road?

The Silk Road and Indian Ocean Trade Network were both critical to international trade, with the Silk Road dominating trade in an earlier period and the Indian Ocean Trade Network somewhat later. The two overlap and interrelate with one another and both illustrate the importance of political stability and traders in maintaining trade, as well as the impact of trade on various communities.

The Silk Road ran East to West across much of the known world. It relied upon ancient roads, many put in place in the Persian Empire as early as 475 BCE. These routes expanded under Alexander the Great in the 4th century BCE. By the 2nd century BCE, this network of roads extended into China, and under the Romans, a more extensive trade network developed. The land-based trade network continued to grow, expand and develop, even as new cultures did. There were several different routes, one to the north, one to the south, and one to the southwest.

Following a brief interruption during the Mongolian Conquest, the Silk Road was reestablished under the Pax Mongolica or Mongolian Peace. The roads were stable and protected, allowing traders to easily move caravans of goods from place to place. From China, porcelain and silk moved into other parts of Asia, North Africa and Europe. Spices and cotton traveled from India and glass and furs from other parts of the world. The most commonly traded goods were small, luxury items that were relatively easy to transport from place to place. Languages, information, culture and religion also travelled along the Silk Road.

Throughout its existence, the Silk Road was impacted by political conditions. When political conditions were stable and the state supported trade, for instance, the Chinese ruling dynasty, it resulted in improved trade along the Silk Road. When conditions were less safe, there was less trade along the Silk Road. Eventually, the Silk Road was largely abandoned as shipbuilding technology, including the Portuguese caravel and the Arabic dhow, improved.

The Indian Ocean Trade Network was somewhat less significant than the Silk Road, but was significantly more stable and less likely to be affected by the actions of local governments. While the Chinese administration was frequently involved in the management of portions of the Silk Road, trade on the Indian Ocean was self-regulated by traders. Local ports could set their own regulations; however, conditions were, on the whole, designed to be favorable for free and profitable trade.

Sea-based trade was typically faster and more efficient than trade over land routes, enabling more extensive trade. The Indian Ocean also offered opportunities for exploration, with both the Chinese and Portuguese expressing interest in that exploration; however, Chinese explorations, led by Zhang He, were terminated by the Ming Dynasty. Eventually, the Portuguese were granted access to West Africa by the Catholic Church. Other noted powers in the region included the Venetians and Ottomans. Later, the British and Dutch controlled trade in the Indian Ocean.

Several differences marked trade between these regions. Often, the same goods were traded by land and sea; however, trade by sea required more investment and was, eventually, largely controlled by a few countries. The Silk Road and land-based trade was less easily managed by large governments and more suited to small-scale trade. It was significantly slower and could move less goods.

3. The "Final Solution" is the name the Nazi party gave to their plan to exterminate the Jews, killing the entire Jewish population of Europe. Today, we commonly refer to this as the Holocaust, the genocide that resulted in approximately 11 million deaths. Identifying the origins of the "Final Solution" poses a number of problems, as, unsurprisingly, the Nazis attempted to hide their intentions, disguised them with euphemisms like "special treatment" and destroyed records wherever possible.

If we begin early in Nazi party history, we find that the Nazis blamed the Jews or a conflation of Jews and communists for the conditions in post-World War I Germany. The anti-Semitic rhetoric of the early days of the party, both before the Munich Beer Hall Putsch and in the early 1930s suggests that there was already, even at this time, a strong desire to eliminate the Jews from Germany and purify the country.

Once the Nazis gained political power in 1933, they had the ability to initiate laws limiting the rights of Jews. Early laws banned Jews from civil service, banned intermarriage, reduced the rights of Jews, including property rights and limited their ability to travel freely, as indicated by the decrees from 1933-1936. Not long after, sterilization laws were initiated. These, while not specifically anti-Semitic, were also intended to purify the German people by eliminating unwanted individuals, including the Roma and the disabled. Not long after, before 1940 as evidenced by the letter from the Reich Minister, euthanasia programs begin, killing disabled children, the mentally ill and even the elderly. The people of Germany did not approve of these programs and the party eventually restructured them to hide their actions. While they hid their plan to kill the unwanted in Germany to avoid negative public opinion, the gas chambers developed in the euthanasia program would be used on a much larger scale in Poland.

While the Wannsee Conference may have defined the "Final Solution" and organized plans for it, this does not, with research, suggest that this was the first plan to destroy the Jewish people. Not long after the invasion of Poland, the Nazis began to move Jewish people into ghettos, limiting not only their right to move freely, but also working to kill them through starvation and disease. It is also clear, in the Goebbels diary, that the "Final Solution" was relatively well-known and not, by all appearances, a shocking revelation to the Nazi administration. Himmler's speech, in fact, suggests that this was not only a public secret among the Nazis, but something he spoke of with great pride.

The implementation of the "Final Solution" relied upon the technology developed during the euthanasia program, gas chambers. They had used gassing vans, first during Operation Barbarossa and later at Chelmno, but this was not adequate for the numbers killed during Operation Reinhard and later in Nazi-occupied Poland. Large-scale gas chambers were built for this purpose. There is one key difference between Auschwitz-Birkenau and the camps of Operation Reinhard. Auschwitz did include a labor camp, and as reflected in the Resettlement document, some individuals were spared immediate execution. Goebbels' letter suggests the use of forced labor as well; however, it would be inaccurate to assume this reflects an intent to spare Jews. Rather, it is more likely an intent to simply work some to death, taking whatever they could before killing them, through deplorable conditions, murder or exhaustion.

Attempts were made, as the war progressed and failure seemed imminent, to hide the evidence of the killing. The opening statements by Robert Jackson at the war crimes trial reflect that fact, as well as the massive amount of evidence collected by the prosecution.

From the first days of the Nazi Party, there was a desire to create a pure German state, free of any sort of racial impurity. The worst of that impurity was, in the eyes of the Nazis, the Jewish people. It is possible that there was some initial intent to simply remove the Jews from Germany, as Jews were free to leave early on, albeit without their property; however, plans to actively deport Jews, like the ghettos of Poland, seem to have been designed to result in the end of the Jewish people, regardless of the factory-style death camps. Those camps made the German plan more practical and efficient, eliminating any need to give space over to the Jews even temporarily.

1. C
2. D
3. A
4. C
5. C
6. D
7. D
8. E
9. A
10. D
11. E
12. E
13. E
14. D
15. C
16. C
17. B
18. B
19. A
20. C
21. B
22. E
23. C
24. B
25. C
26. B
27. E
28. A
29. C
30. D
31. B
32. D
33. E
34. D
35. D
36. A
37. B
38. C
39. C
40. C
41. C
42. A
43. C

44. B
45. C
46. C
47. B
48. C
49. C
50. C
51. B
52. A
53. B
54. C
55. C
56. B
57. B
58. A
59. E
60. D
61. C
62. A
63. A
64. B
65. A
66. B
67. C
68. C
69. C
70. A

1. **How has communist China remained the same and changed over time, from the time of the Chinese Revolution to today.**

At the time of the Chinese Revolution, much of the Chinese population lived rurally and worked in agriculture. There had been foreign communities in China, for instance, in Shanghai; however, these were no longer present by the time of the Chinese Revolution. The nation had suffered horribly since the first invasion by Japan, and continued to throughout World War II. After the war, the nationalist government was quite weak and the civil war ended quickly with a communist victory.

The communist government of the new People's Republic of China set about implementing their social and economic goals and policies almost at once. Mao's Great Leap Forward, introduced in the 1950s was designed to create a modern, loyal and obedient communist state. The goals of the Great Leap Forward included additional industrialization, the collectivization of agriculture, an end to private property, and an end to any potential resistance or rebellion. While the government certainly hoped to create a successful state, the result was a widespread famine, at least in part, manufactured by the activity of the state. Between 18 and 45 million died within just a few years between 1958 and 1961 as the result of the Great Leap Forward. The failure of the Great Leap Forward caused Mao to lose power within China; however, he regained this during the Cultural Revolution.

The Cultural Revolution, beginning in 1966, sought to eliminate western influences through the use of re-education and other policies, including prison camps, youth organizations, and a purge of moderate official. Forced labor was common and a more agricultural lifestyle was idealized. After Mao's death in 1976, the party distanced itself from the Cultural Revolution, recognizing the harm it had called.

Faced with overpopulation and economic challenges, China introduced a one-child policy in 1979. While some exceptions were allowed, this policy dramatically reduced population growth. Today, the policy has been relaxed even more; however, the lasting effects have caused new problems. There are concerns about the number of dependents in an aging population, as well as gender imbalances.

Economic change in China began in the late 1970s, under the leadership of Deng Xiaoping. The first modifications allowed for trade with the west, with the means of production under government control. Gradually, property right s increased, and today, individuals and corporations may hold control of means of production. Towns are encouraged to open factories for export and foreign countries are welcomed as investors in Chinese industry. Far more of the population now works in business or industry, rather than agriculture.

While economic restrictions have loosened, political ones remain quite strict. Chinese nationals can and often do travel, but still live with substantial restrictions regarding speaking out against their government, criticizing the government or exercising freedom of speech or religion.

Today, China is one of the most economically successful nations; however, its people still lack basic protections or freedoms. Prison camps, forced labor and poor work conditions remain common in China. Without these personal freedoms, China remains a step away from western nations, and slightly outside of the international community.

2. Compare the impact of colonialism in India and Latin America.

Both the Latin American countries and India experienced colonialism, but each was under the control of a different colonial power and had distinctly different experiences with imperialism. These experiences have altered the development of nations in both regions, creating close ties in some cases and political struggles in others.

The modern states of India, Pakistan and Bangladesh make up the Indian sub-continent. These were all part of the colonial Raj of the British Empire. The Indian sub-continent had a long history, valuable resources, including cotton and spices, and an equally long history of conquest. In ancient times, Alexander the Great reached India before turning back, and during the 13th century, the Mongols conquered much of the region.

The British conquest of India was based on a desire for trading rights and was originally handled not by the state, but by the British East India Company, incorporated in 1600. Britain, over time, established a treaty-based trade monopoly in India. Violence occurred on Indian soil between the British and French during the 18th century Seven-Year' War. While the original trade monopoly was secured voluntarily through treaties, by the middle of the 18th century, the British East India Company relied upon military force to secure control of India. By the 19th century, the British East India Company acted not only as a commercial force, but an administrative one. Following a rebellion in India in 1857, the British nationalized the British East India Company, making India a British colony. The structures put in place under the company remained.

Once the state was under the control of the crown, efforts were made to keep it peaceful and stable, rewarding and educating locals, often in Britain. Local laws and traditions were allowed to remain, rather than being replaced with western ones. Industry, education and infrastructure were developed under the British, with many locals involved in the process. Notably, the British favored Hindus over Muslims for civil service positions. India became independent after World War II; however, Indian language, culture and religion continued throughout the British occupation of India.

The Spanish were primarily responsible for the settlement of Latin America after Columbus' arrival in the Americas. Conditions in the Americas were very different than those in India. While the religion and culture of India remained intact, the native cultures of the Americas were largely destroyed by colonialism.

First and foremost, native populations in the Americas simply didn't survive the colonization process. Many native groups were warrior cultures, and fought hard against the invaders. Faced with better-armed troops on horseback, many died in battle. Even more devastating was the impact of disease, including smallpox. Finally, the Spaniards put the natives to work in mines and on farms, in unacceptable working conditions, typically without the time or ability to care for their own land or families. Mortality was high. Additionally, the Spanish typically did not travel with wives and families, so married and had children with native women. The mestizo or mixed-race class grew, but the native beliefs, practices and language died out.

The Spanish offered only one path to survival for natives. They could not thrive in Spanish society with their own beliefs and language. Survival required that they accommodate the Spanish by learning their language and converting to Christianity. Some elements of traditional practice remain in Latin American Catholicism; however, the religions of the Aztec and other groups disappeared rapidly.

Both Latin America and India experienced colonialism. India was, fundamentally, a valuable trading partner. It had entered into the partnership voluntarily initially, and there was no expectation of the destruction of the people or their culture. The opposite was true in Latin America. The native peoples were enslaved, with no opportunity for advancement or ability to preserve their own culture. Those who lived did so because they assimilated their new culture.

3. In the late 12th and early 13th century, the Mongolian army, under the control and leadership of Genghis Khan, took over much of the known world. The Mongolians were

a pastoral people, particularly known for their skill on horseback. They lived in relatively small groups, ruled by local leaders. They were nomadic, following their animals. Today, life in parts of Mongolia remains relatively similar, as people still use the traditional yurts and still follow their animals. Genghis Khan was the son of one of these leaders. They were not literate and relatively little is known of the origins of the Mongolian peoples. Many of the stories that circulated later, like the story of Prester John told by Marco Polo, were legend and myth, rather than history.

Before his death in 1227, Genghis Khan had gained control of large areas of East Asia, extending into the Eastern parts of Europe in the west and into China toward the east. After this death, his successors continued these campaigns, sacking Baghdad in 1258 and eventually establishing wide-ranging empires from Moghul India to the Yuan Dynasty.

The Mongolians are commonly known for their armies and their brutality. Cities that offered any resistance were sacked and destroyed, as you can see in the manuscript illustration of the sack of Baghdad. In many cases, civilians, including both women and children were killed or enslaved. Taking the wives and children of a fallen enemy further humiliated him, as noted in the quote from Genghis Khan about gathering them to his bosom. Those cities that surrendered and opened their gates to the Mongol army were typically spared and generally relatively well-treated. The enemies of the Khan were not. Harsh and brutal retribution occurred to those who opposed him, including nobles.

While Genghis Khan is most commonly remembered for his brutality, he was, for his people, a relatively humane ruler. He implemented laws that improved the food supply and condemned the kidnapping of women. He introduced improved record-keeping procedures and protected trade. The later Mongolian empires created stable, elegant and tolerant kingdoms, implementing parts of the local cultures in ways that worked best for them. Under later Mongolian rulers, the Silk Road grew and flourished during the Pax Mongolica.

Later rulers were particularly known for their willingness to adapt, a behavior already seen in Genghis Khan's action as a ruler. Marco Polo, who lived in the court of Kublai Khan in Yuan Dynasty China, recorded his willingness to embrace and explore different religions. The reader should, in this, recognize the cultural relativism. We have no reason to believe that Kublai Khan favored Christianity over Buddhism or Islam, but Marco Polo certainly did. The various Mongol Khans had interactions with Christians, including representatives of the papacy, but would only consider a vassal relationship with these entities. For the Khans, they were the head of the universe and all others, including the Catholic Church, were to provide service to them.

Eventually, the smaller empires fell, one after another. Genghis Khan divided his empire after his death, and the smaller empires could not retain control. While today the Mongolian nation remains, even the final traces of the Mongol empire, the Moghul state of India, eventually fell to the British.

1. D
2. D
3. E
4. D
5. D
6. E
7. B
8. C
9. D
10. C
11. C
12. B
13. C
14. E
15. B
16. B
17. A
18. B
19. C
20. C
21. D
22. E
23. D
24. C
25. A
26. B
27. D
28. C
29. B
30. C
31. B
32. B
33. A
34. D
35. B
36. C
37. E
38. B
39. B
40. A
41. A
42. B
43. B

44. B
45. A
46. C
47. C
48. B
49. C
50. B
51. C
52. D
53. A
54. B
55. A
56. B
57. D
58. C
59. A
60. D
61. B
62. C
63. D
64. B
65. B
66. B
67. E
68. A
69. C
70. C

1. **How have interactions between the United States and other western powers and Japan changed over time and how have the cultural differences and values remained the same?**

Following a long history of isolationism, Japan began regular contact with western powers under the Meiji Restoration in the middle of the 19th century. Japan began an intensive program of modernization at this time, including both the creation of a western-style army and navy and modernizing relatively traditional industries, including the production of porcelain and silk. Between 1868, when the emperor was restored to power, and 1912, Japan changed dramatically. By 1912, it had technology, a military, industry, and infrastructure comparable to those in Western Europe. Japan had already fought and won two wars, one against Russia.

The empire was organized around the emperor; however, actual political power was in the hands of a small elite. Nonetheless, the cult surrounding the emperor formed a critical basis for Japanese civilization. The ideology of loyalty, sacrifice and honor is an essential one to understand later Japanese actions, including aggressive expansionism and the strict discipline of the Japanese military. While there was a cult of the emperor, Japan took repeated steps toward representative democracy early in the 20th century, including universal male suffrage.

As Japan extended its reach early in the 20th century, European powers pushed back, preventing the advancement of the Japanese as a colonial power. After a period of economic recession around the end of World War I, slightly earlier than the Great Depression reached America and Europe, Japan began aggressive action against China. This aggression reached remarkable levels, including horrifying brutality against civilians in Nanjing. The Japanese continued their aggressive plan of expansion, moving outward as World War II began. The Japanese army and pilots were known for their bravery, even in the face of invincible odds. This was supported by the cult of the emperor and the traditional values of Japanese society.

Eventually, this push outward and campaign of aggression led to the bombing of Pearl Harbor. With this, America entered World War II and eventually, with the atomic bomb, defeated Japan. After the war, the west, and America in particular, rebuilt Japan, focusing on Japanese industry. The occupation of Japan continued until 1952; however, America and Japan have remained close since that time. The goal of the occupation was to create a state that was economically strong and stable, but which relied upon outside powers for defense and could not rebuild militarily.

Concerns about Japan's remilitarization were overwhelmed by containment plans for communism, as the Chinese communists created the People's Republic of China. When the final treaties were signed, they were remarkably favorable to the Japanese, with limited penalties for their war crimes. Beginning in 1960, the Japanese have actively worked to embrace Japanese culture, while still thriving in a westernized marketplace.

2. **Compare the impact of the communist revolutions in Russia and China on the people of these countries.**

During the course of the 20th century, both Russia and China experienced communist revolutions, leading to communist systems of government. The revolutions themselves were quite different, but the results held some significant similarities. In more recent history, the two countries have diverged significantly, leading to a distinctly different experience for the population of each country.

The Russian Revolution lasted approximately two years, and was quite violent. After a number of battles, the victory went to the Bolsheviks. Relatively quickly, Vladimir Lenin established a stable government; however, after his death, conditions in Russia were volatile. There were several years of conflict in the communist party, followed by the victory of Josef Stalin.

Under Stalin, the state was strictly authoritarian. There was no room for or tolerance for variation of opinion or ideology. Broad campaigns began to destroy all potential opponents. In some cases, this took the form of murder, with individuals arrested and killed or sent to prison camps, while in others the process was less clear cut.

In the Ukraine, Stalin instituted harsh policies regarding wheat quotas. These quotas had to be met before the people were fed or even had seed grain for the next year. This process, called the holodomor, is often considered a genocide. Millions died of starvation in the Ukraine, even as grain was grown and available.

Conditions in the Soviet Union remained quite harsh under Stalin's rule. Following Stalin's death, there was still relatively little room for opposition. The country was fully industrialized, but the quality of life was quite poor for much of the population. Economic reforms, beginning with perestroika, led to a progressive loosening of restrictions and eventually, the collapse of the Soviet Union.

The Chinese Revolution was a slower process, beginning as a civil war in the years prior to World War II, followed by a break during the war years. After the war, the civil war came to an end rather quickly, with a victory by the communist party. While Stalin had focused on heavy industry, Mao Zedong was primarily concerned with agriculture.

During the "Great Leap Forward" farms were collectivized and grouped into giant facilities. Workers took their meals in dining halls, and lacked any personal incentive for hard work. This failed, miserably, eventually leading to a reversal. While a poor harvest was the result of this, mass starvation also occurred, with events very much like those in the Ukraine in the 1930s. Millions died of starvation, even though, in the cities, warehouses of food were available.

Just as Stalin had culled the intellectuals and westerners, Mao's government did the same. Some were killed outright and many others were sent to re-education camps. The economy was primarily agricultural. Smaller farms took the place after the failure of the "Great Leap Forward" with some ability for individuals to improve their lot in life.

While the Soviet Union collapsed rather than successfully relaxing the economic tenets of communism, China has followed a very different path. China has kept some of the principles of the communist state, including the authoritarianism embraced under Mao, but has relaxed elements of its economic policy, allowing for private property and ownership, including the ownership of factories. The Chinese authorities have sought out western investors and China has, in the last 20 years, become an economic powerhouse. For many people in China, this has provided an improved standard of living, particularly as the working population decreases; however, many in the countryside remain agricultural.

3. Heian Japan marks the end of the classical period in Japanese history. It was a period of remarkable culture, particularly among the elite and it was a time of creative energy, with a new, particularly Japanese identity developing. The Japanese were distancing themselves from Chinese culture and working to create a uniquely Japanese culture, including the incorporation of Pure Land Buddhism. Perhaps most interestingly, this is a period of significant creativity for women, with many women writing about their experiences and lives.

During the Heian period, many women remained relatively isolated. Their actions were controlled by social norms and they typically hid their faces behind large fans or silk and bamboo screens. In court, however, women shed their fans and walked openly, as recorded in the diaries of Sei Shonagan. This woman, like others of the court, was a poet. Whether openly or behind the scenes, women in Heian Japan wielded social power and many were well-educated, with the ability to write poetry. Reciting and writing poetry was considered an attractive trait. While marriages were typically arranged for political gain, affiars were well-tolerated, as shown by the passage by Lady Murasaki. Children born outside of marriage were not considered illegitimate. The first novel, the Tale of Genji by Lady Murasaki, was written by a noblewoman during this time. Her novel illustrates the significant role women played in Heian society, as well as the lively and educated society in which they lived.

In Confucian China, daughters were considered a burden, but in the families of Heian Japan, daughters provided potential access to the imperial family and the only means of social improvement. Before and after this period, female children were frequently exposed at birth, but during this time, daughters were desirable. . They could be married or become concubines, potentially bearing a son to the imperial family. The culture was uxorial with men commonly living with their wives after marriage, providing the wife's family with significant control of her children. The verse written by one of the Fujiwara illustrates this. His daughter has brought honor to his family. Japanese women began to appear, not only in society, but in art, as shown in the illustration of the Tale of Genji.

The growing role of women was supported by the changing religious views of the time. Buddhism was embraced, but integrated aspects of traditional Japanese religion, Shintoism. The strong appreciation of beauty and nature expressed by Sei Shonagan reflects this syncretism. It is also visible in the lotus sutra, a particularly popular sutra during this period. Texts supported the idea that women could become Buddhas without being reborn as men. In this, men and women were equal.

The relative egalitarianism of Heian Japan ended with introduction of the Shogunate and military rule. Women lost their freedom and most were no longer educated. Obedience was valued over the elegant ability to compose poetry at will and recite traditional verses. The writings of women of this time, written in kana, or Japanese script, remain accessible, providing an image into a window of Japanese culture so very different from the culture that followed.

Answer Key 4

1. B
2. A
3. B
4. C
5. A
6. D
7. B
8. E
9. D
10. B
11. A
12. E
13. C
14. B
15. A
16. A
17. E
18. B
19. A
20. E
21. B
22. D
23. C
24. B
25. C
26. D
27. C
28. A
29. B
30. A
31. A
32. C
33. B
34. D
35. C
36. D
37. C
38. D
39. B
40. E
41. A
42. D
43. D

44. A
45. E
46. A
47. D
48. C
49. A
50. C
51. D
52. C
53. D
54. D
55. B
56. A
57. B
58. B
59. C
60. C
61. D
62. D
63. A
64. B
65. D
66. D
67. C
68. E
69. C
70. C

1. **How has Islam changed or remained the same, in terms of action, expectation, beliefs, and values, since its inception in 622 CE?**

Islam was founded by the prophet Muhammad in 622 CE. During the course of his lifetime, Muhammad experienced a number of prophetic visions and experiences, recorded in the written text, the Qur'an. The Qur'an provides a clear guide to life and conduct for Muslims.

Because it is a strongly text-based faith, some aspects of Islamic faith have remained steady throughout time. The Five Pillars of Islam, including the hajj, or pilgrimage to Mecca, donations to the poor, and regular, five times-a-day prayer are unchanging throughout Islam, regardless of where you go or the branch of Islam. The reasoned moderation encouraged in these pillars is also consistent. For instance, pregnant women are not expected to fast during Ramadan, but may make a charitable donation or postpone their fast to a more appropriate time in their lives. The fundamental practices of the faith demonstrate continuity.

Islam has, however, changed significantly. While there was only one branch of Islam originally, today there are two, often in conflict with one another. Shi'a Islam has traditionally been associated with fundamentalism; however, it is more accurate to recognize Shi' as a tradition directly descended from Muhammad and his family members, with clear allegiances to individual spiritual leaders. Sunni Islam has traditionally been considered more moderate and changeable, but today, Sunni Islam is associated with particularly violent political movements in the Middle East.

The role and status of women has also changed in Islamic society. Traditionally, in many Islamic cultures, women lived a relatively public life. They assisted in family businesses, sold goods at market and otherwise participated in the world around them. There is no evidence that they wore the niqab, or black covering over the body, head and face. While the Qur'an speaks of modesty for both men and women, this attire is not required by Islam, but is often required by the Islamic state, for instance, the Taliban government formerly in power in Afghanistan. In many regions, women are denied education, when traditionally many women were quite educated. The first degree-granting university, founded in Muslim North Africa, was the work of a female scholar and there are noted female poets, doctors and mystics in Islamic tradition.

Another clear change in the Islamic faith is the treatment of foreigners. Traditionally, Islam accepted individuals of other religions, first those religions of the book, Judaism and Christianity, but later Hinduism as well. Individuals were free to practice their own faiths, but were required to pay an additional tax. Today, that tolerance is dissipating in many Islamic countries, particularly those embracing Sharia or Islamic law. While Islam was an expansionist religion, spreading rapidly along trade routes, this spread did not involve forced conversions. Acts of terror, like the 9/11 attack and other actions of Al-Quaeda, are not in line with the teachings of the Qur'an.

Islam has retained the traditional practices of prayer, pilgrimage and fasting, but has, in many modern Islamic countries, set aside its traditions of learning, tolerance, and support for women that existed historically. For centuries, Islam protected the knowledge of the classical world, created works of art and helped the world move forward into a brighter and more scientific world. Today, fundamentalist movements, including the Taliban and ISIS, have replaced knowledge and learning with destruction to their own lands, monuments and people.

2. **Compare the Abbasid Caliphate to Western European society in the Middle Ages.**

The world of the Middle Ages encompasses both Western Europe and the empires further east including the Islamic Caliphate. The experiences and environments of these two regionswere utterly different during this period.

The Abbasid Caliphate was the largest Islamic state during the period we commonly define as medieval or the Middle Ages. From around 750 onward, the Abbasid Caliphate created a culturally and intellectually rich empire, known for its learning. In 767, the Abbasids founded the city of Baghdad, later to become a key stop along the Silk Road and a noted center of trade. While the political power of the Abbasid Caliphate was relatively short-lived, it retained cultural and religious power for much longer.

The period from the founding of Islam through the sack of the city by the Mongols in 1258 is commonly referred to as the Golden Age of Islam. The Abbasid Caliphate is at the center of that period, culturally. The government invested in and sponsored learning. They set up hospitals and universities, required medical licenses for doctors, translated classical texts and established lasting trade relations.

After the sack of Baghdad in 1258, the Abbasid Caliphate regained power; however, the Golden Age had come to an end. The Caliphate itself formally came to an end as the region fell under Ottoman control in the 15th century.

While the Abbasid Caliphate was building universities and studying science, the west was fundamentally still, during the Early Middle Ages, in a period often called the dark ages. Literacy was uncommon and technology nearly unknown. Much of the learning of the classical world had been entirely lost and this was a period of significant decline. Cities had shrunk or disappeared, and the Church had little influence in many areas. A few larger local rulers managed to organize to stop the Islamic push into Europe at the French border. Only gradually, in the 9th century, did civilization begin to return to the region. Under Charlemagne, many converted to Christianity and new churches were built, along with monasteries and schools in the cities to train priests. Slowly and gradually, the cities grew. Nonetheless, access to books was minimal and there were few surviving classical texts.

With the support of the Church, the Crusades began. There were several reasons for the Crusades, both pragmatic and religious. Most importantly, however, the wars for control of Jerusalem and surrounding lands brought Christians into close contact with Muslims. While there were no lasting gains of land in the Crusades and no real financial or spiritual gains, the contact between Christians and Muslims brought something critically important to Europe; learning. The classical texts, scientific learning, education and medicine of the Arab world dramatically changed science, learning and even theology in Europe. After this time, the universities grew and blossomed. More men entered the church and the universities and more books were copied and produced.

The cultural interactions of the Crusades helped bring Europe into the High Middle Ages, marked by soaring cathedrals and theology influenced by Aristotelian ideals. While this time was the end of the Golden Age of Islam that was the result of invaders from the East, rather than the Crusades. Both the Golden Age of Islam and the Europe in the High Middle Ages and Renaissance embraced learning and intellectual endeavors as part of a newer, more modern world.

3. In the ancient and medieval world, Africa made up only one part of a broad trading network. Coastal cities were active trading ports, while towns inland were stops along the Sand Road through Africa. While there was a slave trade, it was relatively small in scope. After the discovery of the Americas, that trade in slaves along the West Coast of

Africa increased immensely, destroying the population in some parts of Africa. While attitudes turned against slavery over time, the overall perception of Africa did not change for quite some time. The damage of slavery, colonialism and imperialism remains in Africa even today.

European explorers, like the British Richard Eden, shared his own descriptions of Africans; however, there is no disrespect in his text. These are traders, and even, in his telling, good ones. He was an explorer sharing stories of his explorations and the people he met. The 16th century wholly predates the British desire for imperialism or colonialism. This is clear in Eden's description.

By the late 17th century, slavery was well-established, with huge numbers of slaves captured, kidnapped and sent overseas. While the majority of the slave traders were Portuguese, other Europeans were certainly involved and aware of the slave trade. The European observer identifies those responsible for kidnapping, but does not condemn the act of slavery. He does identify the actions of those who kidnapped their neighbors and associates as treachery, but not the actions of the European slave traders. By the middle of the 18th century, the abolitionist movement was growing, in part, thanks to texts like this one. Alexander Falconbridge wrote his own experiences as a doctor on a slave ship, sharing the inhuman and horrifying conditions on the ship. Published texts like this helped to ban slavery in Britain. While some spoke out against slavery, slavery and imperialism are two distinct and different issues.

The slave trade required a belief, fundamentally, that Africans were less human than people of European origin. While Europe eventually deemed slavery unacceptable and immoral, by the time this occurred, the era of imperialism was beginning. European countries divided up Africa into a number of colonies, each governed somewhat differently. Rudyard Kipling's The White Man's Burden is the epitome of the European attitude in this period. Efforts to colonize, settle and civilize Africa were economically successful, but were also an attempt to illustrate and prove the very quality of European society over African. While interactions between Europeans in Africa were typically peaceful, local people were certainly involved in and damaged by violent conflicts, like the Boer War, as well as by the lasting impact of colonialism in a direct way. Apartheid in South Africa, in which the white population direly limited the rights of Africans through the 1980s and into the 1990s is perhaps the best example of this.

Finally, The Black Man's Burden, written in response to Kipling's poem, provides an end statement to the era of imperialism. This shows the costs of imperialism. Even today, these costs remain as ethnic groups and different regions battle with one another and countries struggle to establish peaceful and stable governments.

Made in the USA
San Bernardino, CA
20 August 2018